LIQUID EXPLORATIONS

Grades 1-3
(with modifications for kindergarten)

Skills
Observing, Comparing, Describing, Classifying,
Recording, Drawing Conclusions

Concepts
Properties of Liquids

Themes
Systems & Interactions, Stability, Patterns of Change,
Structure, Matter

Mathematics Strands
Logic, Pattern, Measurement, Number

Nature of Science and Mathematics
Scientific Community, Interdisciplinary, Cooperative Efforts,
Science & Society, Real-Life Applications

Time
Five or more class sessions

Leigh Agler

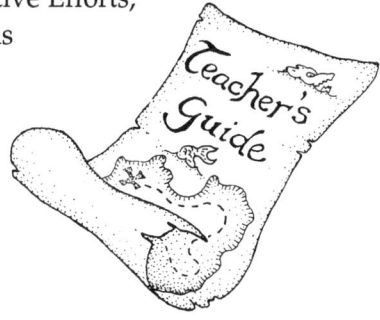

LHS GEMS

Great Explorations in Math and Science (GEMS)
Lawrence Hall of Science
University of California at Berkeley

Visit the GEMS Web site at
www.lhsgems.org or e-mail us at
gems@uclink4.berkeley.edu

Illustrations
Carol Bevilacqua
Lisa Klofkorn

Photographs
Richard Hoyt

Lawrence Hall of Science, University of California,
Berkeley, CA 94720. Chairman: Glenn T. Seaborg
Director: Marian C. Diamond

Initial support for the origination and publication of the GEMS series was provided by the A.W. Mellon Foundation and the Carnegie Corporation of New York. GEMS has also received support from the McDonnell-Douglas Foundation and the McDonnell-Douglas Employees Community Fund, the Hewlett Packard Company Foundation, and the people at Chevron USA. GEMS also gratefully acknowledges the contribution of word processing equipment from Apple Computer, Inc. This support does not imply responsibility for statements or views expressed in publications of the GEMS program. Under a grant from the National Science Foundation, GEMS Leader's Workshops have been held across the country. For further information on GEMS leadership opportunities, or to receive a publication brochure and the *GEMS Network News*, please contact GEMS at the address and phone number below.

©1986 by The Regents of the University of California. All rights reserved. Printed in the United States of America. Reprinted with revisions 1989, 1991, 1993, 1995, 1997, 2001, 2004.

International Standard Book Number: 0-924886-62-5

COMMENTS WELCOME

Great Explorations in Math and Science (GEMS) is an ongoing curriculum development project. GEMS guides are revised periodically, to incorporate teacher comments and new approaches. We welcome your criticisms, suggestions, helpful hints, and any anecdotes about your experience presenting GEMS activities. Your suggestions will be reviewed each time a GEMS guide is revised.
Please send your comments to:
GEMS Revisions, c/o Lawrence Hall of Science, University of California, Berkeley, CA 94720.
The phone number is (510) 642-7771.

Great Explorations in Math and Science (GEMS) Program

The Lawrence Hall of Science (LHS) is a public science center on the University of California at Berkeley campus. LHS offers a full program of activities for the public, including workshops and classes, exhibits, films, lectures, and special events. LHS is also a center for teacher education and curriculum research and development.

Over the years, LHS staff have developed a multitude of activities, assembly programs, classes, and interactive exhibits. These programs have proven to be successful at the Hall and should be useful to schools, other science centers, museums, and community groups. A number of these guided-discovery activities have been published under the Great Explorations in Math and Science (GEMS) title, after an extensive refinement process that includes classroom testing of trial versions, modifications to ensure the use of easy-to-obtain materials, and carefully written and edited step-by-step instructions and background information to allow presentation by teachers without special background in mathematics or science.

Staff

Glenn T. Seaborg, Principal Investigator
Jacqueline Barber, Director
Kimi Hosoume, Assistant Director
Cary Sneider, Curriculum Specialist
Katharine Barrett, Kevin Beals, Ellen Blinderman,
Beatrice Boffen, John Erickson, Jaine Kopp, Laura Lowell,
Linda Lipner, Debra Sutter, Rebecca Tilley, Laura Tucker,
Carolyn Willard, Staff Development Specialists
Jan M. Goodman, Mathematics Consultant
Cynthia Eaton, Administrative Coordinator
Karen Milligan, Distribution Coordinator
Lisa Haderlie Baker, Art Director
Carol Bevilacqua and Lisa Klofkorn, Designers
Lincoln Bergman, Principal Editor
Carl Babcock, Senior Editor
Kay Fairwell, Principal Publications Coordinator
Nancy Kedzierski, Felicia Roston, Vivian Tong,
Stephanie Van Meter, Staff Assistants

Contributing Authors

Jacqueline Barber
Katharine Barrett
Kevin Beals
Lincoln Bergman
Celia Cuomo
Philip Gonsalves
Jaine Kopp
Linda Lipner
Laura Lowell
Linda De Lucchi

Jean Echols
Jan M. Goodman
Alan Gould
Kimi Hosoume
Susan Jagoda
Larry Malone
Cary I. Sneider
Debra Sutter
Jennifer Meux White
Carolyn Willard

Reviewers

We would like to thank the following educators who reviewed, tested, or coordinated the reviewing of this series of GEMS materials in manuscript form. Their critical comments and recommendations contributed significantly to these GEMS publications. Their participation does not necessarily imply endorsement of the GEMS program.

ARIZONA

David P. Anderson
Royal Palm Junior High School, Phoenix

Joanne Anger
John Jacobs Elementary School, Phoenix

Cheri Balkenbush
Shaw Butte Elementary School, Phoenix

Flo-Ann Barwick Campbell
Mountain Sky Junior High School, Phoenix

Sandra Caldwell
Lakeview Elementary School, Phoenix

Richard Clark*
Washington School District, Phoenix

Kathy Culbertson
Moon Mountain Elementary School, Phoenix

Don Diller
Sunnyslope Elementary School, Phoenix

Barbara G. Elliot
Tumbleweed Elementary School, Phoenix

Joseph M. Farrier
Desert Foothills Junior High School, Phoenix

Mary Anne French
Moon Mountain Elementary School, Phoenix

Leo H. Hamlet
Desert View Elementary School, Phoenix

Elaine Hardt
Sunnyslope Elementary School, Phoenix

Walter Carroll Hart
Desert View Elementary School, Phoenix

Tim Huff
Sunnyslope Elementary School, Phoenix

Stephen H. Kleinz
Desert Foothills Junior High School, Phoenix

Alison Lamborghini
Orangewood Elementary School, Phoenix

Karen Lee
Moon Mountain Elementary School, Phoenix

George Lewis
Sweetwater Elementary School, Phoenix

Tom Lutz
Palo Verde Junior High School, Phoenix

Midori Mits
Sunset Elementary School, Phoenix

Brenda Pierce
Cholla Junior High School, Phoenix

Sue Poe
Palo Verde Junior High School, Phoenix

Robert C. Rose
Sweetwater Elementary School, Phoenix

Liz Sandberg
Desert Foothills Junior High School, Phoenix

Jacque Sniffen
Chaparral Elementary School, Phoenix

Rebecca Staley
John Jacobs Elementary School, Phoenix

Sandra Stanley
Manzanita Elementary School, Phoenix

Chris Starr
Sunset Elementary School, Phoenix

Karen R. Stock
Tumbleweed Elementary School, Phoenix

Charri L. Strong
Mountain Sky Junior High School, Phoenix

Shirley Vojtko
Cholla Junior High School, Phoenix

K. Dollar Wroughton
John Jacobs Elementary School, Phoenix

CALIFORNIA

Carolyn R. Adams
Washington Primary School, Berkeley

Judith Adler*
Walnut Heights Elementary School, Walnut Creek

Gretchen P. Anderson
Buena Vista Elementary School, Walnut Creek

Beverly Braxton
Columbus Intermediate School, Berkeley

Dorothy Brown
Cave Elementary School, Vallejo

Christa Buckingham
Seven Hills Intermediate School, Walnut Creek

Elizabeth Burch
Sleepy Hollow Elementary School, Orinda

Katharine V. Chapple
Walnut Heights Elementary School, Walnut Creek

Linda Clar
Walnut Heights Elementary School, Walnut Creek

Gail E. Clarke
The Dorris-Eaton School, Walnut Creek

Sara J. Danielson
Albany Middle School, Albany

Robin Davis
Albany Middle School, Albany

Margaret Dreyfus
Walnut Heights Elementary School, Walnut Creek

Jose Franco
Columbus Intermediate School, Berkeley

Elaine Gallaher
Sleepy Hollow Elementary School, Orinda

Ann Gilbert
Columbus Intermediate School, Berkeley

Gretchen Gillfillan
Sleepy Hollow Elementary School, Orinda

Brenda S.K. Goo
Cave Elementary School, Vallejo

Beverly Kroske Grunder
Indian Valley Elementary School, Walnut Creek

Kenneth M. Guthrie
Walnut Creek Intermediate School, Walnut Creek

Joan Hedges
Walnut Heights Elementary School, Walnut Creek

Corrine Howard
Washington Elementary School, Berkeley

Janet Kay Howard
Sleepy Hollow Elementary School, Orinda

Gail Isserman
Murwood Elementary School, Walnut Creek

Carol Jensen
Columbus Intermediate School, Berkeley

Dave Johnson
Cave Elementary School, Vallejo

Kathy Jones
Cave Elementary School, Vallejo

Dayle Kerstad*
Cave Elementary School, Vallejo

Diane Knickerbocker
Indian Valley Elementary School, Walnut Creek

Joan P. Kunz
Walnut Heights Elementary School, Walnut Creek

Randy Lam
Los Cerros Intermediate School, Danville

Philip R. Loggins
Sleepy Hollow Elementary School, Orinda

Jack McFarland
Albany Middle School, Albany

Betty Maddox
Walnut Heights Elementary School, Walnut Creek

Chiyomi Masuda
Columbus Intermediate School, Berkeley

Katy Miles
Albany Middle School, Albany

Lin Morehouse*
Sleepy Hollow Elementary Schoool, Orinda

Marv Moss
Sleepy Hollow Elementary School, Orinda

Tina L. Neivelt
Cave Elementary School, Vallejo

Neil Nelson
Cave Elementary School, Vallejo

Joyce Noakes
Valle Verde Elementary School, Walnut Creek

Jill Norris
Sleepy Hollow Elementary School, Orinda

Janet Obata
Albany Middle School, Albany

Patrick Pase
Los Cerros Intermediate School, Danville

Geraldine Piglowski
Cave Elementary School, Vallejo

Susan Power
Albany Middle School, Albany

Louise Rasmussen
Albany Middle School, Albany

Jan Rayder
Columbus Intermediate School, Berkeley

Masha Rosenthal
Sleepy Hollow Elementary School, Orinda

Carol Rutherford
Cave Elementary School, Vallejo

Jim Salak
Cave Elementary School, Vallejo

Constance M. Schulte
Seven Hills Intermediate School, Walnut Creek

Robert Shogren*
Albany Middle School, Albany

Kay L. Sorg*
Albany Middle School, Albany

Marc Tatar
University of California Gifted Program, Berkeley

Mary E. Welte
Sleepy Hollow Elementary School, Orinda

Carol Whitmore-Waldron
Cave Elementary School, Vallejo

Vernola J. Williams
Albany Middle School, Albany

Carolyn Willard*
Columbus Intermediate School, Berkeley

Mary Yonekawa
The Dorris-Eaton School, Walnut Creek

KENTUCKY

Joyce M. Anderson
Carrithers Middle School, Louisville

Susan H. Baker
Museum of History and Science, Louisville

Carol Earle Black
Highland Middle School, Louisville

April B. Bond
Rangeland Elementary School, Louisville

Sue M. Brown
Newburg Middle School, Louisville

Donna Ross Butler
Carrithers Middle School, Louisville

Stacey Cade
Sacred Heart Model School, Louisville

Sister Catherine, O.S.U.
Sacred Heart Model School, Louisville

Judith Kelley Dolt
Gavin H. Cochran Elementary School, Louisville

Elizabeth Dudley
Carrithers Middle School, Louisville

Jeanne Flowers
Sacred Heart Model School, Louisville

Karen Fowler
Carrithers Middle School, Louisville

Laura Hansen
Sacred Heart Model School, Louisville

Sandy Hill-Binkley
Museum of History and Science, Louisville

Deborah M. Hornback
Museum of History and Science, Louisville

Patricia A. Hulak
Newburg Middle School, Louisville

Rose Isetti
Museum of History and Science, Louisville

Mary Ann M. Kent
Sacred Heart Model School, Louisville

James D. Kramer
Gavin H. Cochran Elementary School, Louisville

Sheneda Little
Gavin H. Cochran Elementary School, Louisville

Brenda W. Logan
Newburg Middle School, Louisville

Amy S. Lowen*
Museum of History and Science, Louisville

Mary Louise Marshall
Breckinridge Elementary School, Louisville

Theresa H. Mattei*
Museum of History and Science, Louisville

Judy Reibel
Highland Middle School, Louisville

Pamela R. Record
Highland Middle School, Louisville

Margie Reed
Carrithers Middle School, Louisville

Donna Rice
Carrithers Middle School, Louisville

Ken Rosenbaum
Jefferson County Public Schools, Louisville

Edna Schoenbaechler
Museum of History and Science, Louisville

Karen Schoenbaechler
Museum of History and Science, Louisville

Deborah G. Semenick
Breckinridge Elementary School, Louisville

Dr. William McLean Sudduth*
Museum of History and Science, Louisville

Rhonda H. Swart
Carrithers Middle School, Louisville

Arlene S. Tabor
Gavin H. Cochran Elementary School, Louisville

Carla M. Taylor
Museum of History and Science, Louisville

Carol A. Trussell
Rangeland Elementary School, Louisville

Janet W. Varon
Newburg Middle School, Louisville

MICHIGAN

Glen Blinn
Harper Creek High School, Battle Creek

Douglas M. Bollone
Kelloggsville Junior High School, Wyoming

Sharon Christensen*
Delton-Kellogg Middle School, Delton

Ruther M. Conner
Parchment Middle School, Kalamazoo

Stirling Fenner
Gull Lake Middle School, Hickory Corners

Dr. Alonzo Hannaford*
Western Michigan University, Kalamazoo

Barbara Hannaford
The Gagie School, Kalamazoo

Duane Hornbeck
St. Joseph Elementary School, Kalamazoo

Mary M. Howard
The Gagie School, Kalamazoo

Diane Hartman Larsen
Plainwell Middle School, Plainwell

Miriam Hughes
Parchment Middle School, Kalamazoo

Dr. Phillip T. Larsen*
Western Michigan University, Kalamazoo

David M. McDill
Harper Creek High School, Battle Creek

Sue J. Molter
Dowagiac Union High School, Dowagiac

Julie Northrop
South Junior High School, Kalamazoo

Judith O'Brien
Dowagiac Union High School, Dowagiac

Rebecca Penney
Harper Creek High School, Battle Creek

Susan C. Popp
Riverside Elementary School, Constantine

Brenda Potts
Riverside Elementary School, Constantine

Karen Prater
St. Joseph Elementary School, Kalamazoo

Joel Schuitema
Woodland Elementary School, Portage

Pete Vunovich
Harper Creek Junior High School, Battle Creek

Beverly E. Wrubel
Woodland Elementary School, Portage

NEW YORK

Frances P. Bargamian
Trinity Elementary School, New Rochelle

Barbara Carter
Jefferson Elementary School, New Rochelle

Ann C. Faude
Heathcote Elementary School, Scarsdale

Steven T. Frantz
Heathcote Elementary School, Scarsdale

Alice A. Gaskin
Edgewood Elementary School, Scarsdale

Harriet Glick
Ward Elementary School, New Rochelle

Richard Golden*
Barnard School, New Rochelle

Seymour Golden
Albert Leonard Junior High School, New Rochelle

Don Grant
Isaac E. Young Junior High School, New Rochelle

Marybeth Greco
Heathcote Elementary School, Scarsdale

Peter C. Haupt
Fox Meadow Elementary School, Scarsdale

Tema Kaufman
Edgewood Elementary School, Scarsdale

Donna MacCrae
Webster Magnet Elementary School, New Rochelle

Dorothy T. McElroy
Edgewood Elementary School, Scarsdale

Mary Jane Motl
Greenacres Elementary School, Scarsdale

Tom Mullen
Jefferson Elementary School, New Rochelle

Robert Nebens
Ward Elementary School, New Rochelle

Eileen L. Paolicelli
Ward Elementary School, New Rochelle

Donna Pentaleri
Heathcote Elementary School, Scarsdale

Dr. John V. Pozzi*
City School District of New Rochelle, New Rochelle

John J. Russo
Ward Elementary School, New Rochelle

Bruce H. Seiden
Webster Magnet Elementary School, New Rochelle

David B. Selleck
Albert Leonard Junior High School, New Rochelle

Lovelle Stancarone
Trinity Elementary School, New Rochelle

Tina Sudak
Ward Elementary School, New Rochelle

Julia Taibi
Davis Elementary School, New Rochelle

Kathy Vajda
Webster Magnet Elementary School, New Rochelle

Charles B. Yochim
Davis Elementary School, New Rochelle

Bruce D. Zeller
Isaac E. Young Junior High School, New Rochelle

DENMARK

Dr. Erik W. Thulstrup
Royal Danish School of Educational Studies, Copenhagen

*Trial test coordinators

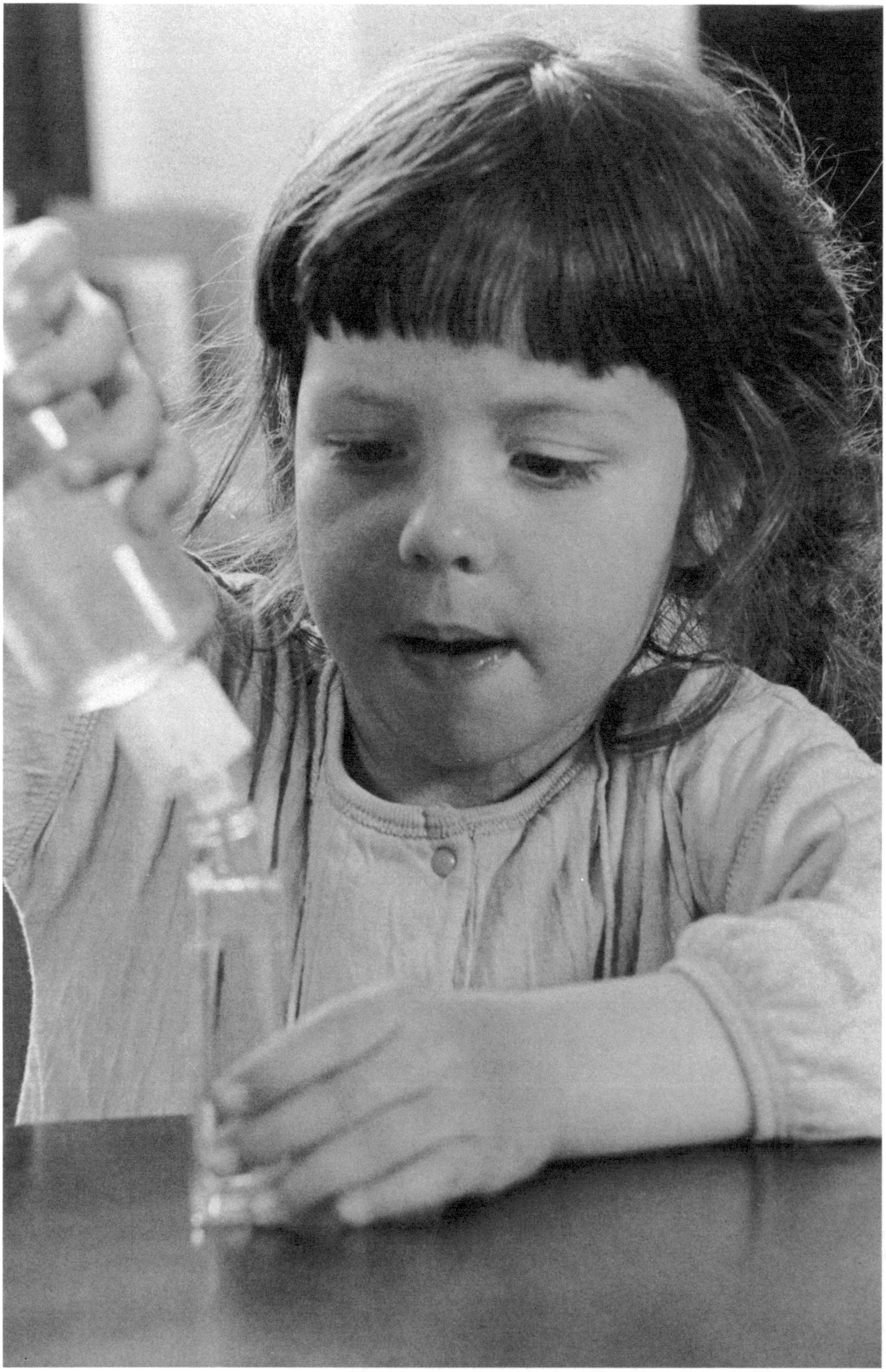

Contents

Acknowledgement viii
Introduction 1
Time Frame 3
Activity 1: Liquid Classification Game 5
Activity 2: Swirling Colors 15
Activity 3: Raindrops and Oil Drops 25
Activity 4: Ocean in a Bottle Demonstration 33
Activity 5: Secret Salad Dressing 39
Summary Outlines 50
Assessment Suggestions 58
Resources 59
Literature Connections 61
Helpful Hints for Hands-On Science in the Classroom 65

Acknowledgments

The activities in this unit were developed by Leigh Agler, Jacqueline Barber, Kimi Hosoume, and Geri Martin, staff of the Lawrence Hall of Science Chemistry Education Department. Thanks as well to Laura Lowell and Jacqueline Barber for their assistance with the 1995 revision of this guide. Lillian Weber from City College of New York provided the inspiration for "Raindrops and Oil Drops." Special thanks go to the GEMS reviewers and their students for all the contributions that "bubbled up" from their experiences with these activities, and we also offer a pink lemonade toast to all teachers who are able to "go with the flow" enough to take on this "all wet" unit. Cheers!

Introduction

From the water we drink to the oceans that encompass the globe, liquids are everywhere and are used in countless ways. *Liquid Explorations* provides rich experiences in physical science for primary students as they observe and experiment with various liquids. In this series of five activities, your students learn about important qualities of liquids as they develop skills in observing, describing, comparing, classifying, recording observations, and drawing conclusions.

In the first activity, the students are introduced to the properties of liquids in an engaging game. They develop classification skills as they examine different liquids and describe the qualities that make one liquid different from another. After they describe these qualities, and have developed a need for more sophisticated vocabulary, definitions of *liquid* and *property* are offered. Next, they observe, compare, and record the way food coloring moves through different liquids. In the third activity, your students discover that some liquids mix while others do not. This fundamental concept is reinforced and extended throughout the unit from watching colors swirl in pink lemonade, to creating an "ocean in a bottle" and a "secret salad dressing."

"Summary Outlines" are provided to help you guide your students through these activities in an organized way. Possible modifications for younger students are also included at the end of each activity. You will also find some "Literature Connections" at the end of the guide to help you expand your students' experience with liquids through literature and the language arts.

The goal of this unit is to give children a chance to explore and enjoy the properties of liquids as they develop science skills. In the future your students will learn the scientific principles behind many of the phenomena they observe in these activities. On first exposure it is best that they not be overburdened by abstract explanations and technical terms such as: surface tension, polarity, miscibility, and density. If you do choose to introduce vocabulary words or simplified explanations, limit them to descriptions of what your students can see. In later years your students will be better able to understand explanations of the phenomena if they have seen and described them in your science class.

A month before starting this unit, have your students begin a collection of the many bottles and jars needed. "Helpful Hints For Hands-On Science," on page 61, has a sample letter to parents requesting donations. Refer to this section for additional tips on organizing the materials needed for this unit and for making the activities go smoothly.

Some teachers who have presented these activities decided on "liquids" as the theme for a semester long unit. Others used this unit as the starting point for the study of liquids, solids, and gases. If you would like to continue investigating physical science with your students, we suggest following this unit with the GEMS unit entitled *Involving Dissolving*. By having your students engage in the "Going Further" activities, by extending the scientific investigation techniques in this unit and *Involving Dissolving*, and by adding creative ideas that you and your students suggest, you can delve much further into the properties of various substances. From these initial experiments with liquids can flow an awakened sense of curiosity and wonder about the vast variety of substances in the world around us.

Time Frame

Because of the considerable variation in the time it takes experienced teachers to present these activities, a range of times has been listed. Teachers with varying time constraints have come up with creative ways to adapt the time frame of this unit to their own needs. We suggest that you read each activity and plan where you might break it into another class session if you find that it takes your students longer than you expected.

Activity 1: Liquid Classification
 Initial Teacher Preparation: 30 minutes
 Classroom Activity: several 15–25 minute sessions

Activity 2: Swirling Colors
 Teacher Preparation: 30 minutes
 Classroom Activity: 30–50 minutes

Activity 3: Raindrops and Oil Drops
 Teacher Preparation: 30 minutes
 Classroom Activity: 30–60 minutes

Activity 4: Ocean in a Bottle Demonstration
 Teacher Preparation: 15 minutes
 Class Demonstration: 15–30 minutes

Activity 5: Secret Salad Dressing
 Teacher Preparation: 20 minutes
 Classroom Activity: 40–70 minutes

Complete classroom kits for GEMS teacher's guides—including a **Liquid Explorations GEMS Kit***, as well as refill kits, are available from Sargent-Welch. For further information call 1-800 727-4368 or visit www.sargentwelch.com*

4   Activity 1

Activity 1: Liquid Classification Game

Overview

In this game, the teacher classifies liquids according to a secret rule. The students are challenged to guess the secret rule. At first, several clear containers of liquids are organized into two groups. As you introduce each additional liquid, the students try to determine into which group the liquid belongs. "It goes there because it is clear like those liquids!" "Put it in that group because it is thick and moves slowly!" When your students become familiar with the game, they can take turns classifying the liquids, and you can introduce new ways to classify.

The purposes of this activity are to: (1) provide short, repeated experiences in observing, comparing, classifying, and describing; (2) provide a wide variety of examples to illustrate the definition of a liquid as "something that flows" and (3) help your students become familiar with the various properties of different liquids.

Students who have had experience identifying attributes have an easier time with this game than those who have not. You may want to precede this first session with other activities that give students practice in identifying attributes. (See "Resources" on page 59 for suggestions of several curricula that have lessons on this topic.)

Background

Your students' abilities to classify improve as they mature. Some kindergarten and first grade students may only be able to deal with two liquids at a time, making a one-to-one match based on a single property. As students mature, they will be able to classify a large number of objects based on a single property and to order things serially (e.g., from light to dark or thick to thin).

You can use the classification aspect of this activity to assess the abilities of your students and to give them more experience with classification. Do not feel that you or they have failed if they have difficulty with more advanced levels of classifying. For less mature students, emphasize observing, comparing, and matching. Students of all levels will sharpen their observation powers, develop descriptive language skills, and gain experience comparing a wide variety of liquids. It is interesting to try this same activity at the end of the unit or later in the school year and assess how student classification skills have improved.

What You Need

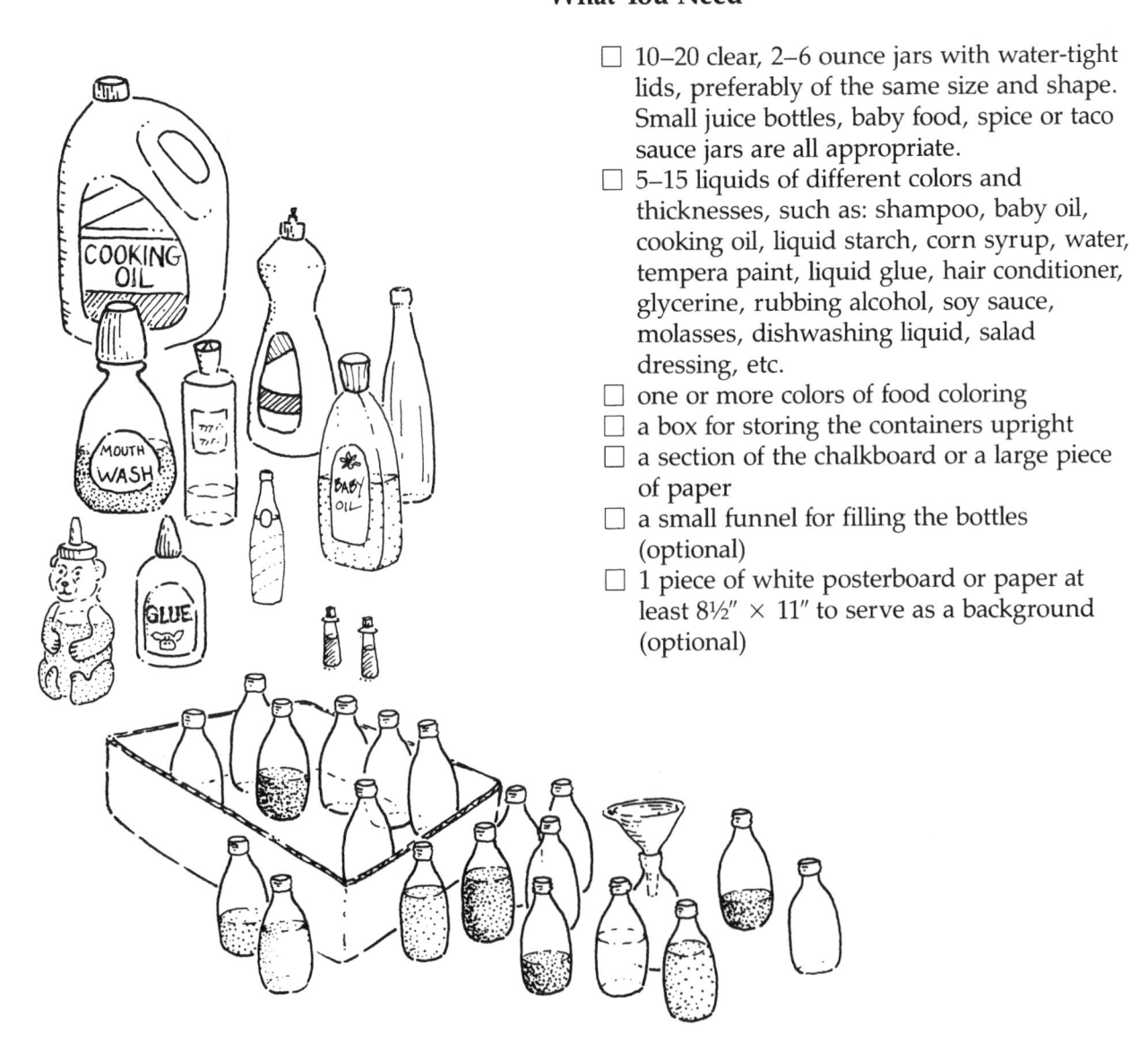

- ☐ 10–20 clear, 2–6 ounce jars with water-tight lids, preferably of the same size and shape. Small juice bottles, baby food, spice or taco sauce jars are all appropriate.
- ☐ 5–15 liquids of different colors and thicknesses, such as: shampoo, baby oil, cooking oil, liquid starch, corn syrup, water, tempera paint, liquid glue, hair conditioner, glycerine, rubbing alcohol, soy sauce, molasses, dishwashing liquid, salad dressing, etc.
- ☐ one or more colors of food coloring
- ☐ a box for storing the containers upright
- ☐ a section of the chalkboard or a large piece of paper
- ☐ a small funnel for filling the bottles (optional)
- ☐ 1 piece of white posterboard or paper at least 8½" × 11" to serve as a background (optional)

Getting Ready

1. At least a month before starting this unit, have your students begin a collection of the many bottles and jars you will need. "Helpful Hints For Hands-On Science in the Classroom" beginning on page 61, includes a sample letter to parents requesting donations. The jars used in this activity can be rinsed out and saved for the next time you teach the activity.

If you are going to use any literature connections for this activity, obtain them. We especially recommend Two Bad Ants. *(See page 63.)*

2. Fill each of the small bottles with the various liquids you have collected. Fill some completely, others halfway, and some one-quarter full. By coloring a liquid, or by choosing a different quantity, the same liquid can be used several times. Do not mix liquids together. You may want to number the jars and make a "key," so you remember what each is. Put the containers of liquids in a box.

3. Write the word "LIQUID" in large letters on a piece of paper or on a nearby chalkboard.

4. Optional: Set up a white sheet of posterboard or paper to serve as a background for the clear containers of liquids. This will make it easier for students sitting farther away to see the liquids.

Activity 1

The most obvious ways of classifying the liquids are:

- *colored/colorless*
- *see-through/not see-through*
- *full/partially full*

Other attributes your students may discover after playing with the bottles themselves are:

- *liquids that stick to the container walls/ those that flow back immediately*
- *red/not red. . . yellow/not yellow*
- *form bubbles/do not form bubbles*
- *makes a noise when shaken/makes no noise*

You may want to post a running list of different ways you and your students classified liquids on a section of chalkboard or on a recording sheet. The classification schemes can be described in words or represented graphically with drawings.

Playing the Game

1. Ask the group to tell you their favorite drinks. Point to the word "liquid" on the chalkboard and tell students that all the things they drink are liquids. Ask the group if they can think of liquids that they don't drink. Tell the class that they will be studying various liquids—how they are similar and how they differ.

2. Take two jars out of the box. Ask the group how their contents are the same. Hold up one or two of the containers and gently move them. Accept all reasonable answers.

3. Line up about 10–15 containers of liquids in front of the students. Select two containers with an easily recognizable similar attribute, such as liquids that are colored, and set them in one place. Put two liquids that are colorless together in another place. Ask the class to find another liquid that would fit in one or the other of these groups. If the liquid they choose for a given group does not follow your rule, put it in the correct group and say, "It goes in this group according to my secret rule."

8 Activity 1

4. When all the liquids have been put in groups, ask the class to guess what rule you used in classifying them. If they don't guess your classification scheme correctly, help them isolate the attribute that is common to all the liquids in one group by asking questions. The discussion that takes place as the students "guess the rule" is one of the high points of the activity. Encourage a full exchange of ideas.

5. Repeat the game, basing your "rules" on one attribute at a time. Continue to play the game, as long as it holds your students' interest.

6. Conclude the activity by asking, "What is the same about all the things in these bottles?" **Use the students' responses to arrive at a definition of a liquid as something that flows.** If necessary, remind the class that *all* the bottles contain liquids, by demonstrating how the contents of all the bottles flow.

Subsequent Sessions

Students enjoy playing this game and it works well when repeated daily for short 10–15 minute sessions. Many teachers have set up a station in the room so that students may manipulate and classify the liquids independently.

1. Remind the students how the liquids were classified in previous sessions. Then choose another way of classifying the liquids and play a round of the game.

2. Invite a student to devise a rule for grouping the liquids. Have a student first whisper his idea to you, and if it is reasonable, help him classify four to six liquids. Have the class try to guess his rule. Students commonly repeat a classification the teacher has introduced. That's okay. Give several students a chance to invent a rule.

3. Conclude by asking what the contents of all the jars have in common.

If you get too many "wrong" answers, assume that your class is not ready for this level of classifying, and change the game to one of the simpler versions suggested in the Classification Levels section on page 10.

This definition obviously has some limitations (for example, sand and salt also "flow") but it is a good working definition for students of this age doing these activities. More refined definitions of liquids, solids, and of gases develop in later grades. The GEMS assembly presenter's guide Solids, Liquids, and Gases explores this subject for upper elementary students.

Your students may ask you whether things like pancake batter or a thick milk shake are liquids. While these are not liquids in the strict sense of the word, since they contain solid particles in suspension, for the purposes of this unit, a liquid is defined as "something that flows." A good way to respond might be to ask them if they think pancake batter flows.

Observing your students as they play the liquid classification game before, during, and after the unit could serve as an excellent assessment.

Classification Levels

Following are variations of the classification game in order of increasing complexity. Look for the level where the majority of your students are most successful and interested.

- **Level 1: Matching by given property.** Line up all of the containers. Choose one to place in front of the line. Challenge students to find one other liquid that best matches this one according to one property that you name, such as color or thickness.

- **Level 2: Matching by mystery property.** Line up all of the containers and choose one to place in front. Without stating a specific property, challenge students to choose another liquid that goes with it in some way. Have each student tell how the two liquids are alike. Provide plenty of time, so several different responses can be given.

- **Level 3: Classifying into two groups.** Increase the number of liquids students classify into two groups, as described previously.

- **Level 4: Classifying into more than two groups.** Classify the liquids into more than two groups, such as, colorless, light colored and dark colored, or low, medium and high liquid levels.

- **Level 5: Serial Classification.** Introduce serial classification by creating a line of many liquids that varies from left to right according to one characteristic. (For example, light to dark, or small amount to full.)

Going Further

- As a class project, make a bar graph showing the popularity of your students' favorite beverages.

- Make lists of "drinkable" and "non-drinkable" liquids as part of a safety lesson.

- Your students will be curious about the contents of the jars. Respond to this curiosity by conducting a guessing game that focuses on careful observation. Post a list of the liquids you used, provide time for students to manipulate and observe the mystery liquids, then poll the students to see which liquid they think is in each jar before revealing the correct answer.

- Students love to bring mystery liquids from home. Send a note home to parents, asking them to give their child some liquid in a tightly-closed clear container, preferably plastic. Caution them not to allow their child to bring in poisonous or caustic liquids. Allow time for the students to manipulate each mystery liquid and guess its identity based on their observations.

- Play the classification game again but this time have your students classify solids. **Solids can be defined simply as "things that hold their shape," or "things that you cannot put your finger through."** Such simplified definitions are good starting points for primary students.

- Provide your students with other materials to classify, such as leaves, attribute blocks, fruits and vegetables, or shoes.

- Have your students make a mural or collage of liquids using drawings and magazine pictures. Or start a museum of liquids in a corner of your room, inviting students to bring in things from home to add to the "liquid museum."

Our favorite drinks

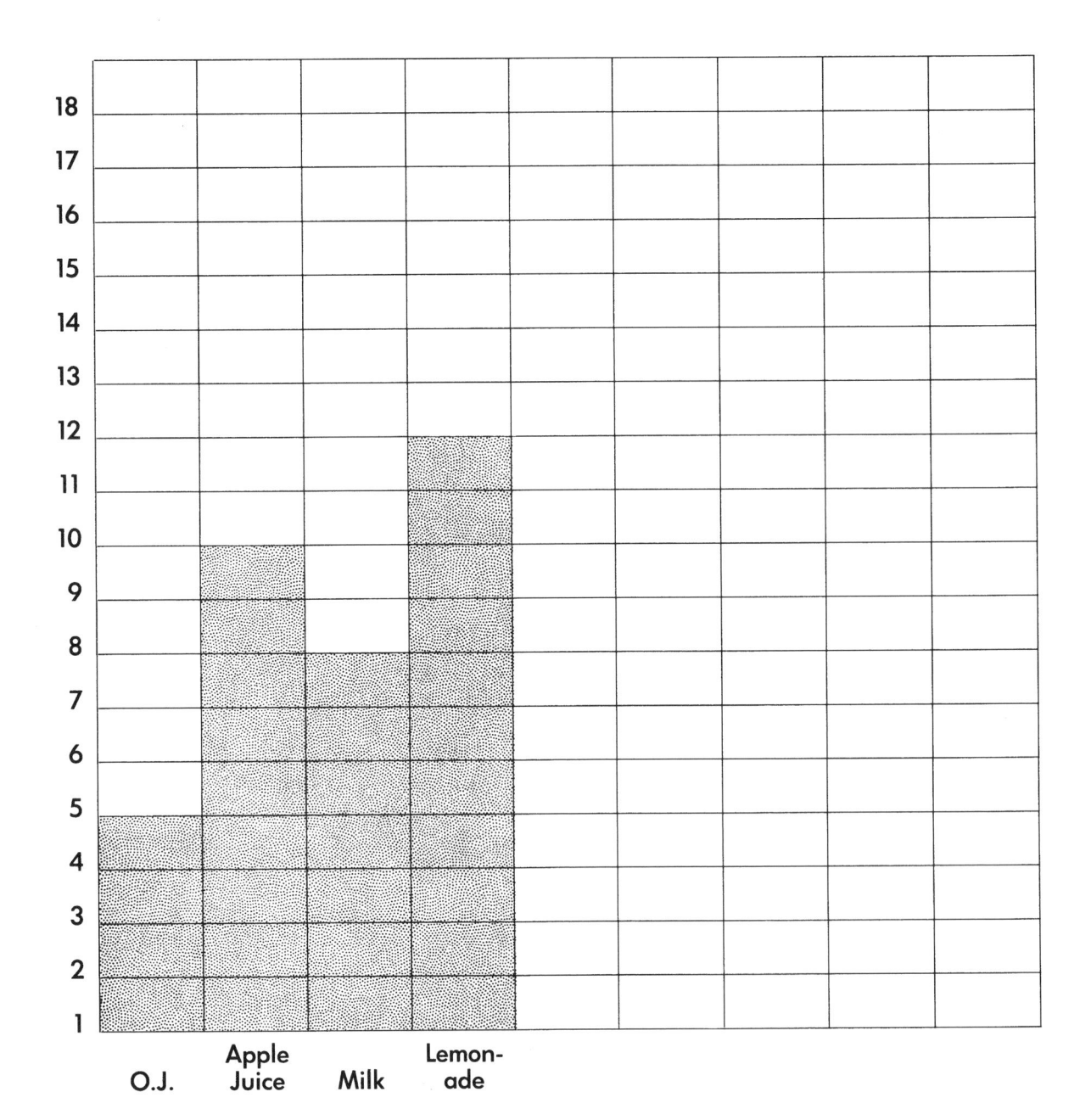

	O.J.	Apple Juice	Milk	Lemonade
Votes	5	10	8	12

12 Activity 1

Modifications for Kindergarten

• Precede the liquid classification game by allowing your students to classify objects that are easier to distinquish, such as attribute blocks, buttons, or their shoes.

• Compare solids and liquids when introducing the word "liquid."

• Simplify the level of classifying you use with younger students. Use the first two variations described in the Classification Levels section on page 10. If the class is successful at these, then go on to the method described above.

• Allow more opportunities for students to manipulate and classify the liquids by themselves.

• If the word "flow" is unfamiliar to your students, you may wish to define a liquid as "something that will pour." Be aware that using this simpler definition may lead to confusion if one of your students points out that sand will pour. While sand does pour one grain at a time, it does not flow continuously like a liquid.

14   *Activity 2*

Activity 2: Swirling Colors

Overview

A drop of food coloring glides gently through a glass of water, making beautiful streamers and swirls of color. But try adding a drop of food coloring to a glass of *salt* water—the color patterns you will see are totally different! In this activity, your students have an opportunity to observe, record, and compare the patterns of color made in various liquids. They discover that some liquids that may appear the same are actually very different. The students conclude their investigations with a refreshing surprise—a glass of pink lemonade.

What You Need

For the class:
- ☐ 1 pitcher, 2–4 quart capacity (2–4 liters)
- ☐ 1 clear wide-mouthed container, 2–4 quart capacity (2–4 liters). A large glass jar or the bottom cut from a 2-liter clear, plastic, colorless soda bottle will work.
- ☐ 3 quart or liter bottles of salt-free seltzer water
- ☐ 2 lemons
- ☐ 1 knife (for cutting lemons)
- ☐ ¾ cup sugar
- ☐ container to hold sugar
- ☐ 1 tablespoon
- ☐ 1 plastic stir stick (coffee stirrers or popsicle sticks work well)
- ☐ 1 long-handled spoon
- ☐ 1 squeeze bottle of red food coloring
- ☐ 1 squeeze bottle of blue food coloring
- ☐ 1 blank piece of paper
- ☐ 1 bucket, or access to a sink
- ☐ paper towels or sponges
- ☐ a chalkboard or a large piece of paper

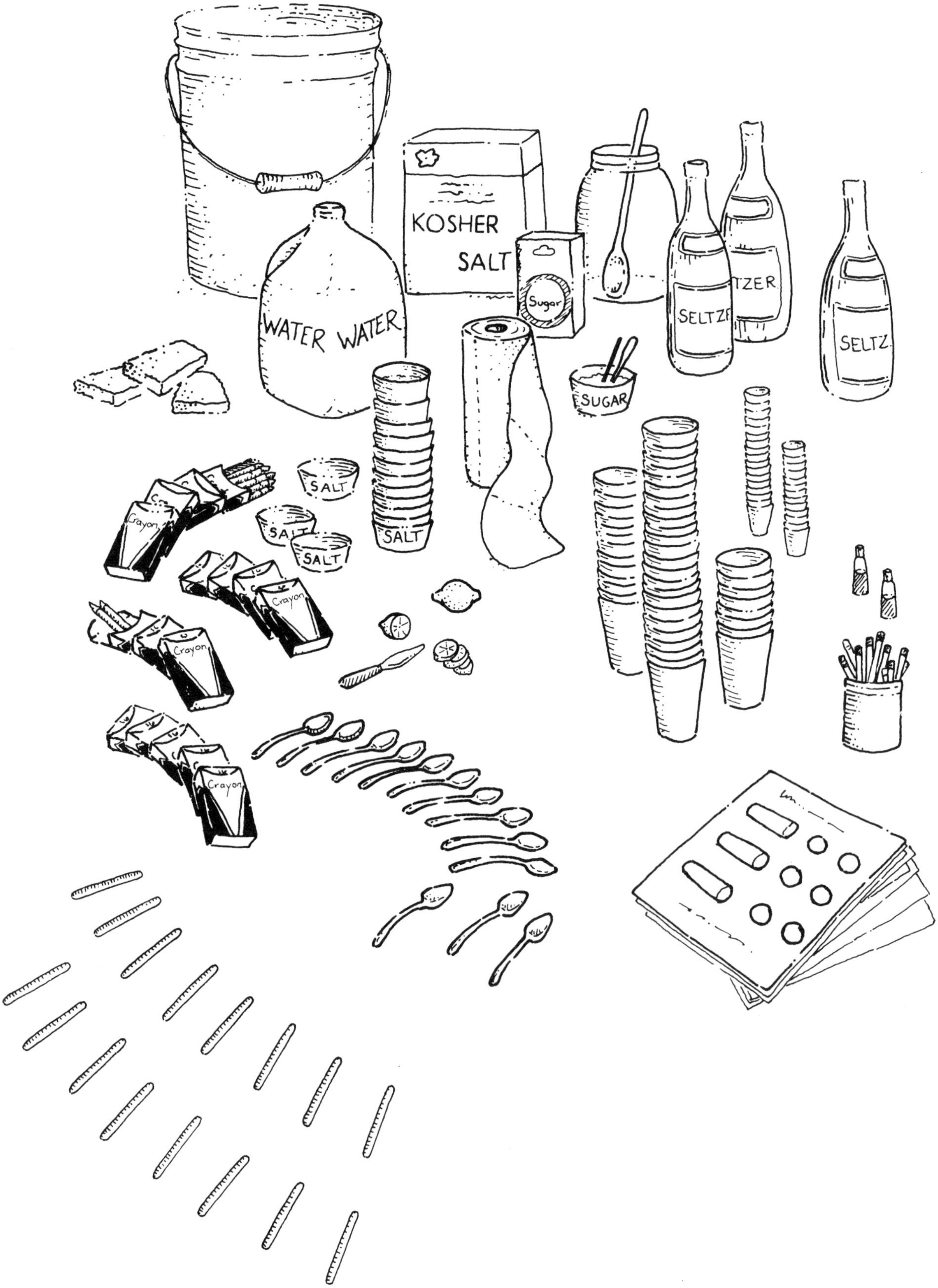
KOSHER
SALT
Sugar
WATER WATER
SELTZER
TZER
SELTZ
SUGAR
SALT
SALT
SALT
SALT
Crayon
Crayon
Crayon
Crayon

For each pair of students:
- ☐ 3 tall, clear plastic cups, 10-ounces (the taller the cup, the better the opportunity to see the downward pattern of the swirls)
- ☐ 2 small paper cups
- ☐ 1 container for salt, such as a margarine tub or other wide-mouthed, squat container
- ☐ 5 teaspoons kosher or pickling salt (kosher or pickling salt are preferable because when dissolved they leave no visible trace. The additives in most other varieties of table salt cause water to look cloudy. If additive-free salt is unavailable, any table salt will work.)
- ☐ 1 plastic stir stick
- ☐ 1 teaspoon-sized spoon
- ☐ 2 crayons
- ☐ 2 pencils
- ☐ 2 "Swirling Colors" data sheets, master included, page 23

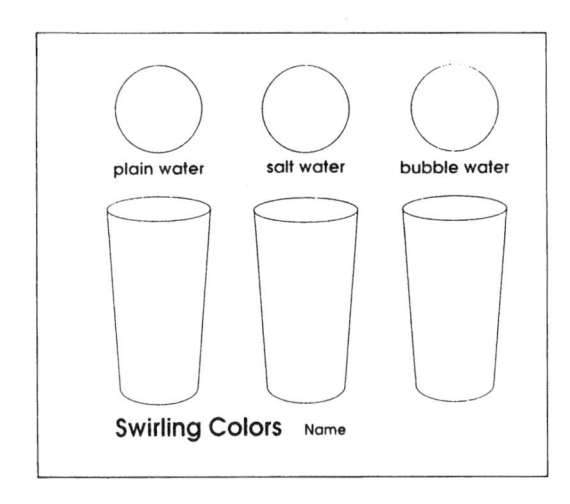

Getting Ready

1. Duplicate one copy of the "Swirling Colors" data sheet for each student from the master on page 23.

2. For each pair of students, fill one salt container with approximately 5 teaspoons of salt. Place a stir stick and teaspoon in each container.

3. Arrange desks in pairs. Place a data sheet and a crayon at each desk. Place three cups on the data sheet at one desk and a salt container on the other desk.

4. Fill the pitcher with water and use it to fill the first two cups on each desk three-quarters full with water.

5. Fill the large, clear container with approximately two quarts of water. Place this container, the sugar, tablespoon, long-handled spoon, food coloring, a blank sheet of paper, a crayon, and paper cups near where you will introduce the activity.

6. Sketch the shape of the large container filled with water on the blank sheet of paper.

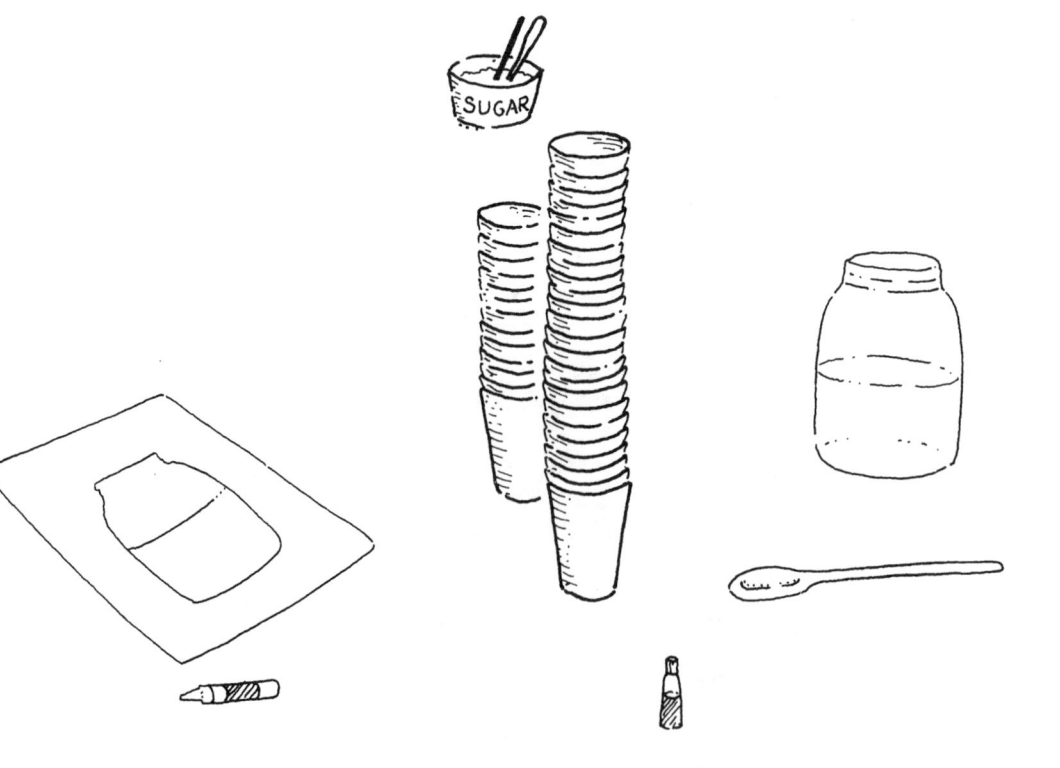

Introducing the Activity

1. Gather the students away from their desks. Explain to them that in this activity they'll observe the ways in which drops of food coloring move through various liquids.

2. Demonstrate how to use a stir stick to level spoons of sugar as you measure 8 tablespoons into the large, clear container. Stir the solution until the students say they can no longer see the sugar. Explain that although the water looks the same, it has changed. It is now sugar water.

3. Have the class tell you when the sugar water stops moving. Ask your students to predict what might happen if you add one drop of red food coloring to the surface of the liquid. Then add one drop of the food coloring to the surface. Have your students watch what happens. Emphasize the importance of not jiggling, stirring, or blowing on the liquid. (This sugar water is the beginning of the surprise pink lemonade that concludes this activity.)

4. Hold up the sketch of the water container so all students can see it. Place a crayon where you added your food coloring. Ask a volunteer to describe what she noticed after you first added the drop to the water. As she talks, move the crayon accordingly to draw the trail left by the drop.

5. Tell the class that the drawing shows the way food coloring moves through sugar water. They will watch how a drop of food coloring moves through plain water, salt water, and bubbly water. Have students raise their hands to indicate whether they think the trails will look different or the same in the three liquids.

6. Explain to the students that they will be working in pairs. One student will keep the cups in front of him on the paper. The other student will measure and stir. Both students will get to record what happens to the drop, with a crayon on a data sheet.

7. Tell your students that the first liquid they will investigate is plain water, so they should not add any salt to it. The second liquid they'll investigate is salt water. Before you add a colored drop to their plain water, they'll need to make their salt water.

8. Explain that after they've made their salt water, you will go around adding a drop of coloring to each of their plain-water cups. The students should draw what they notice when the drop is placed in the cup. **It is important to stress that they should begin drawing as soon as the color is dropped in their cups.**

9. Have your students return to their seats and write their names on their data sheets.

Observing and Recording

1. Ask each person to place her hand over the **middle** cup. Explain that this cup has to be ready so that the liquid will not be moving when they use it later. Tell the "measurers" to carefully measure four teaspoons of salt into this **middle** cup and then stir it until they can't see the salt.

2. Remind the class that the first cup is the plain water and that they should begin drawing as soon as you put a colored drop in the water. Circulate around the room, placing a drop of blue food coloring in each cup of plain water. Allow time for all students to draw. After about a minute, ask all students to put down their crayons (the food coloring continues to mix over time, so the swirling effect is lost when all the water in the cup turns blue). You might want to have two or three students collect the salt containers, stir sticks, and spoons, as you distribute the food coloring, so students aren't tempted to engage in additional experiments.

3. Ask a volunteer to describe what they observed as the blue drop moved through the water. Did anyone else notice the same thing?

4. Ask your students to raise their hands if their salt water is still. Tell the class to carefully draw what they see when you add the colored drop to the cup containing the salt water. Add a drop to each salt water cup, **reminding students to draw what they see right away.**

5. While the students are drawing, open the seltzer bottles. When your students are ready, fill each team's third cup half-full with the bubbly water and then go around adding a drop of food coloring. Remind your students to begin drawing immediately.

Some teachers have students place the three cups in a line next to each other but above or to the side of the student sheet so students can draw two views of each on the sheet itself: the view from the top can be drawn in the circles, and the side-view in the glasses below. Other teachers have students place the three cups in the drawn circles, as shown in the photograph on page 21. Either way is fine.

A Refreshing Finale

1. Bring a bucket around to each team and have them empty their cups into it. Ask the teams to come to the discussion area with their drawings.

2. Draw three cups labeled "plain water," "salt water," and "bubbly water" on the chalkboard. For each liquid, ask two volunteers to hold up their data sheets and describe what they noticed, as you draw their descriptions on the board.

3. Help the class summarize how the different liquids changed the way the food coloring moved. Your students will probably observe that the food coloring will slowly swirl and move through plain water; in salt water it will start to sink and then return to the upper part of the cup; the coloring in the bubbly water will disperse quickly. Even though some of the liquids look similar, what happened to the color shows us that they are different.

4. Squeeze the lemons into the sugar water left from the demonstration. Pour this pink lemonade into paper cups for the students to drink and enjoy!

Some teachers present a "Shipwrecked!" scenario in which a pirate is left on an island with an unknown clear liquid. Presented as a demonstration, you can have three cups in front of the class (and you can pretend to be the pirate). One cup is known to have fresh water, one salt water, and the other is the "mystery liquid." Have students suggest how you could find out whether the mystery liquid is salt water or fresh without tasting it. This can also serve as an assessment of what they've learned through this activity.

Going Further

• Demonstrate how a drop of food coloring will move through other liquids, such as vinegar, oil, milk, or clear apple juice.

• Present your students with a mystery liquid. Have them observe how a drop moves through it. Ask them to compare this with other liquids they tested. In which liquids did the coloring move differently? In which liquids did it move in the same way? Can they identify the liquid?

Modifications for Kindergarten

1. Give the students only one liquid at a time. This will also decrease the number of cups needed.

2. Eliminate the third liquid—seltzer water. It can be presented as a teacher demonstration during the finale.

3. Provide the students with one data sheet for each liquid they use. This will allow them to concentrate on fewer things at once.

4. Young students are often too excited to record the results of what they see. Some teachers have opted to let their kindergarteners observe the swirling colors one day without the need to record. On a subsequent day they repeat the experiment, this time having students record what happens.

plain water

salt water

bubble water

Swirling Colors Name _____

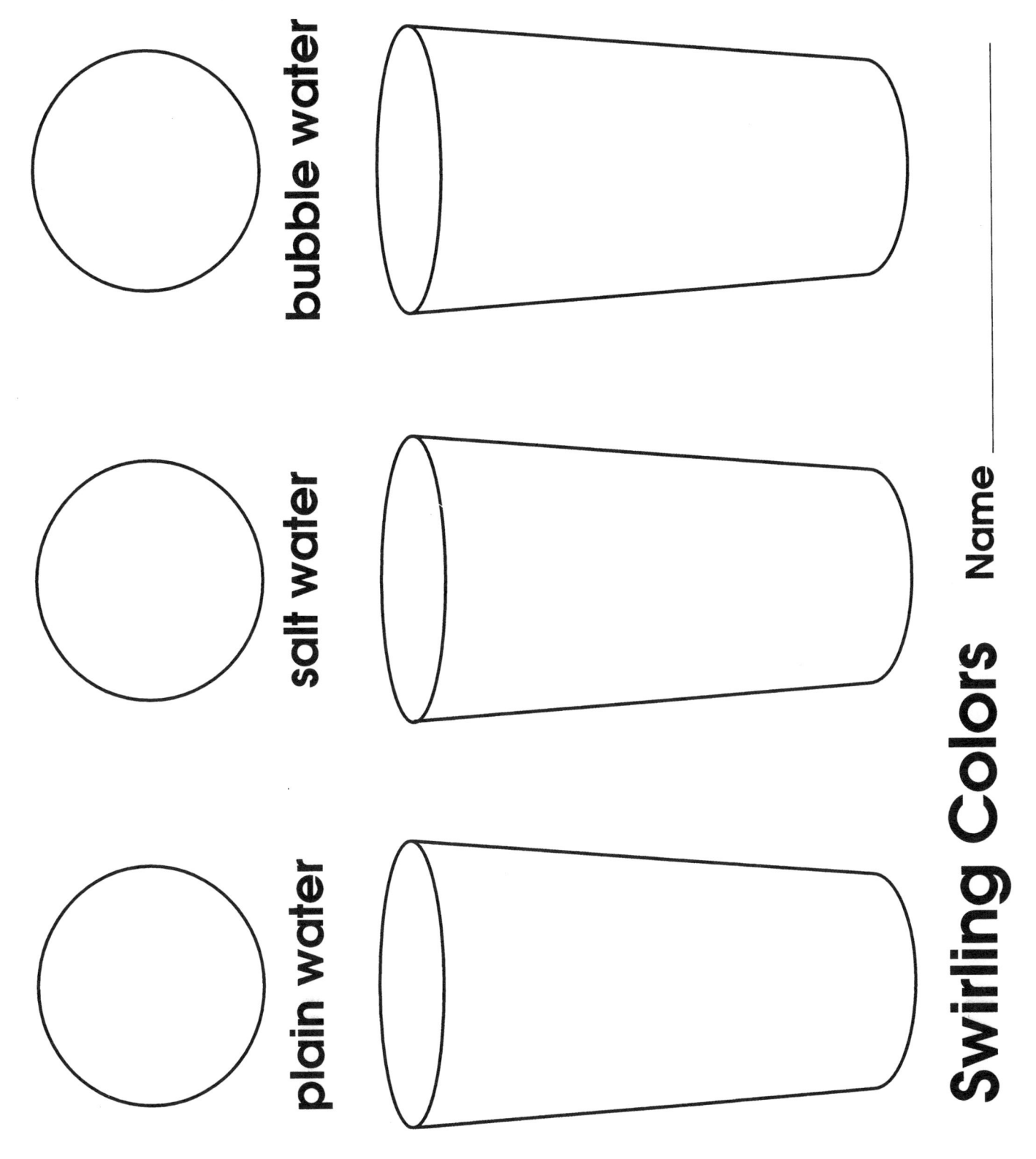

© 1987 by The Regents of the University of California
LHS—Great Explorations in Math and Science: *Liquid Explorations*

Activity 2

24   *Activity 3*

Activity 3: Raindrops and Oil Drops

Overview

In this activity, your students are given the opportunity to play with drops of two very different liquids, and to investigate questions such as: What shape is a water drop? Is an oil drop shaped like a water drop? Can drops be "broken up?" Can they be "stuck together?" Can one drop be floated on another? What are some ways to move drops along a waxed surface? Do drops look the same on all surfaces? This close-up view will sharpen your students' scientific thinking skills and allow them to discover more ways in which liquids are similar and different.

What You Need

For the class:
- [ ] newspaper (enough to cover the tables and some extra)
- [ ] a water bucket, or access to a sink
- [ ] 1 pitcher, 1–2 quart capacity (1–2 liters)
- [ ] 1 clear, 8–10 ounce cup
- [ ] 1 cup of cooking, salad, or baby oil
- [ ] 1 tray
- [ ] several extra paper plates
- [ ] approximately 7 yards of waxed paper
- [ ] a chalkboard or 2 large pieces of paper
- [ ] dishwashing soap, sponges, and paper towels for cleanup

For each pair of students:
- [ ] 1 4–10 ounce container for holding water, such as a paper cup, or a cottage cheese container
- [ ] 1 high-rimmed bottle cap, such as those from vinegar jugs or screw top bottles
- [ ] 2 drinking straws (clear straws are preferable but not essential)
- [ ] 2 9-inch paper plates

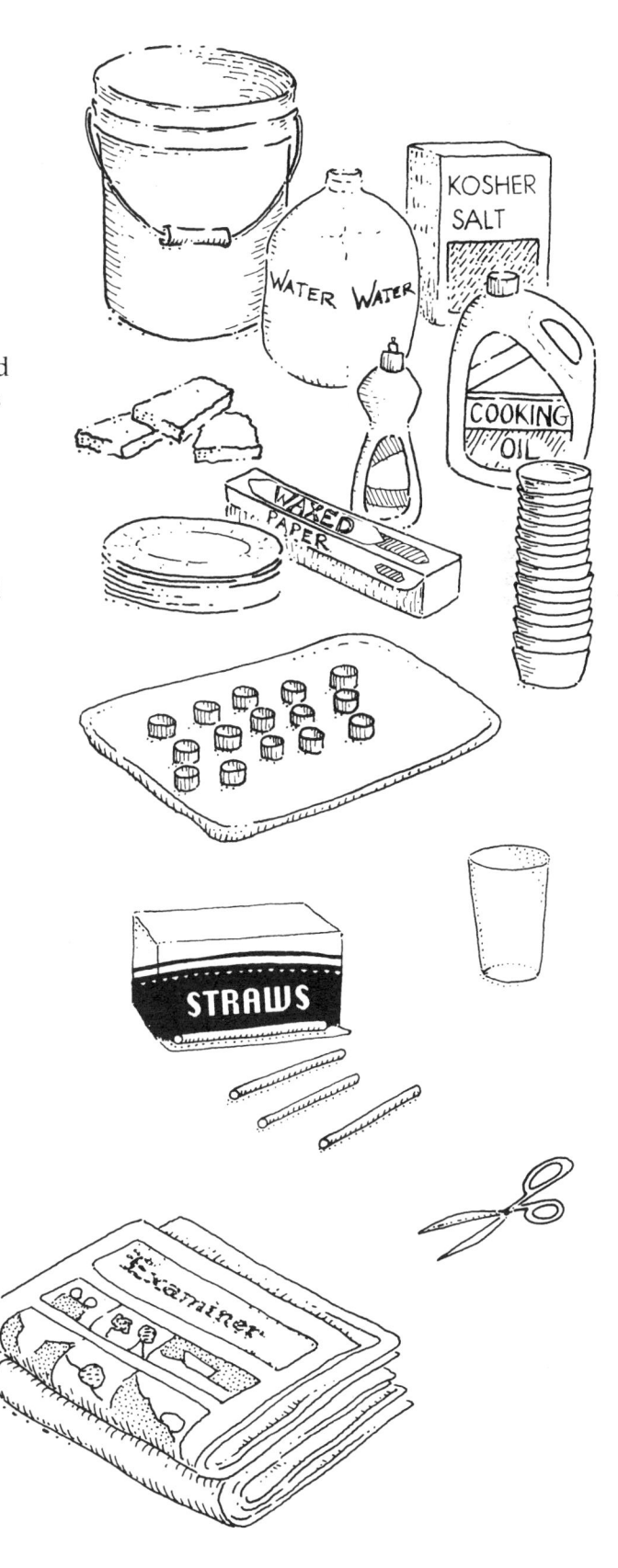

Getting Ready

1. Cut squares of newspaper and waxed paper, each approximately 6" × 6", so there's enough for each child to have one, plus a few extras.

2. Cut the drinking straws in half and remove their wrappers. Practice using a straw-eyedropper as described in "Demonstrating the Dropper" below.

3. Arrange desks in pairs and cover them with newspaper.

4. Put a waxed paper square on a paper plate for each student.

5. If there is no water source in the room, fill a water bucket and use one cup as a dipper to halfway fill all of the cups. Distribute one water container at each pair of desks. Fill a clear cup with water for the introduction.

6. Fill the bottle caps with oil and place these on a tray. (Caps are used because they are hard to spill and hold small enough quantities to make spills manageable.)

7. Place the straws, the cup of water, the bottle of oil, stacks of plates, and the newspaper squares on a table near where you will introduce the activity.

Demonstrating the Dropper

1. Gather the class in an area away from their desks. Hold up the bottle of oil and a cup of water for the class to identify. Ask how these two liquids are different. Explain that they will be observing these liquids closely to find out the shapes of drops, and how drops move.

26   Activity 3

2. Demonstrate to the class how to use a straw as a homemade eyedropper:

    a. Fold over the top third of the straw, and pinch the double portion of the straw (not the fold).

    b. **Keep squeezing** as you lower the straw into the cup of water.

    c. Stop squeezing, then lift the straw out of the cup.

    d. Pinch a little bit at a time to make drops come out.

Some teachers put a piece of tape around the bend in the dropper to make it a little easier for small hands to use.

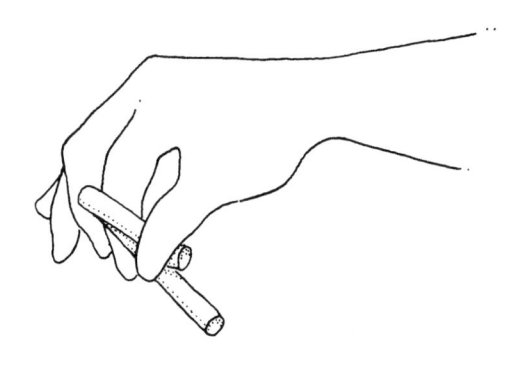

3. Emphasize the need to make a small drop by showing them how to pinch the straw quickly, just once. Show your students how to move their heads down to eye level with the table to get a good look at the drop from the **side**.

4. Tell the students that they will practice using the droppers without water a few times before going to their seats. Hand out one straw to each student. Take the group through the steps one-by-one, reminding them to:

- **Keep squeezing** until the straw is in the water.

- **Stop squeezing** when they are ready to take the straw out of the water.

- **Take the straw out** of the water.

- **Pinch** the straw quickly to make small drops.

Repeat the sequence, using "imaginary water," until most of the students seem to understand how to use a dropper.

5. On the chalkboard, make and label three drawings: a ball shape, a hill (or dome) shape, and a flat pancake shape. Explain that these are pictures of what some drops look like **from the side.** Demonstrate how they will need to view drops from the side by bringing your eyes down to table level. Tell the class that you'd like each person to decide what shape they think looks most like a water drop.

Investigating Water Drops

1. Send the students back to their seats with their straws, a plate, and a waxed paper square. Explain that they will each share a cup of water with a partner.

2. As long as the students have droppers in their hands, it may be difficult to get the attention of the entire class. Instead, circulate among the students, helping them with their droppers and posing questions to help focus their investigations, such as:

- Is the drop shaped like a ball, a dome, or flat like a pancake? Do all of the drops look the same from the side?

- Try moving the drop with your straw. Can you drag it? Can you push it?

- Can you split a drop into smaller drops? Can you push them together to make a bigger one?

3. After ten to fifteen minutes, ask the students to put down their droppers and come to the discussion area or gather around the chalkboard. Tell your students that you'd like to hear what they found out about the water drops. Conduct an opinion poll. Have them raise their hands to indicate the shapes they saw when they looked at their water drops. Write the number of votes each shape received on the chalkboard next to the drawings. Circle the shape most frequently seen.

Some students will want to know what shape water and oil drops are "supposed" to be. It's important to encourage students to be confident in drawing conclusions based on what they observe. One effective way to help students make their own observations is to ask, "What shape were your water drops?" Another way to encourage all students to report their observations is to poll the group. The purpose of polling is not to "vote" for the "right" answer, but to allow every student to describe what they observed.

4. Use the same polling procedure to find out what the students discovered about the questions you asked while they were investigating:

- Raise your hand if you could drag a water drop.
- Raise your hand if you could push one.
- Raise your hand if you could split a water drop into smaller drops.
- Raise your hand if you could push them together to make a bigger drop.

Investigating Oil Drops

1. Tell the group you'd like them to compare what they learned about water drops with oil:

- Does an oil drop have the same shape as a water drop?
- Can oil drops be moved in the same ways as water drops?
- What happens when you try to put a water drop and an oil drop together?
- What happens when you place an oil drop in water?

2. Have students return to their seats and distribute a cap of oil and a new straw-eyedropper to each pair of students.

3. For those students who need additional challenges, distribute squares of newspaper and ask them to compare how the drops look and move on newspaper.

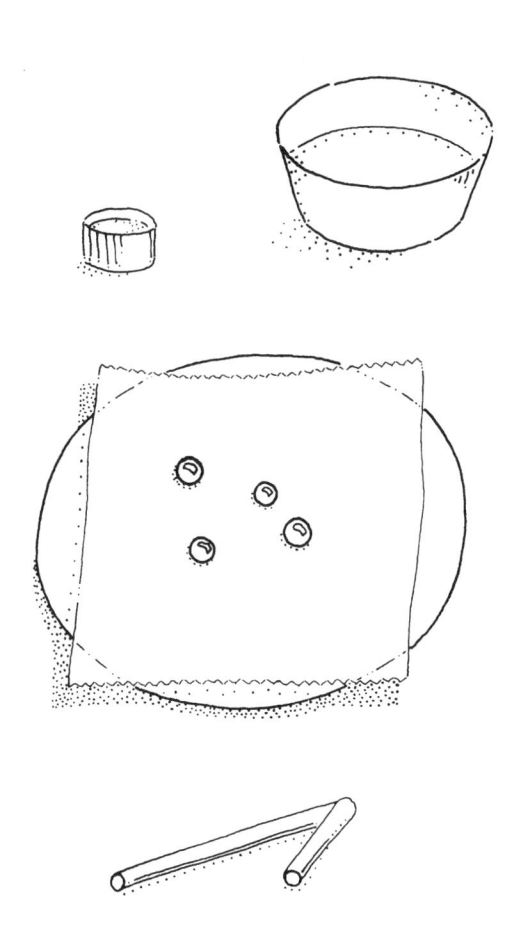

An excellent way to extend the activities in this session is to raise questions about oil spills. Based on their experience, what do your students think happens when a tanker spills oil into the ocean? Where does the oil go? How might it be cleaned up? This session was used by many teachers in Alaska following the large oil spill there, giving students direct experience to help them better understand the news reports they heard. In addition to providing an important real-life connection for their science experiments, learning more about oil spills introduces environmental concerns, and naturally extends into other curriculum areas, such as social studies, reading, writing, and current events.

4. Have the students return to the discussion area or chalkboard. Call on individuals to answer the following questions:

- What shape is an oil drop?

- Does an oil drop look like a water drop?

- What happens when you place an oil drop in water?

- What happens when an oil drop and a water drop are put together?

- Did the drops look the same on newspaper as they did on waxed paper? Did they move in the same way?

Cleanup Tips

1. Bring a pitcher or bucket around to each pair of desks. Empty the water from the cups into the bucket.

2. Collect the caps of oil on a tray. Discard any oil remaining in the caps and soak the caps in soapy water.

3. Have each pair of students roll up the newspaper at their desks with the straws and plates and discard all of it.

Going Further

- Pass around one or more magnifying lenses for students to see. Ask: "What shape is the magnifying lens?" Compare its shape with that of the drops when looked at from the side. The dome shape of the magnifier makes things on the other side appear larger. Have the students try placing a piece of waxed paper over a newspaper square and putting a drop of water on the waxed paper. Does the newsprint appear larger? Have groups of two or three students share materials to simplify this activity.

- Have your students investigate how drops of various liquids (vinegar, salt water, or milk) behave on a number of different surfaces (foil, construction paper, the pavement).

- Challenge your students to count the number of drops that can be piled on a penny without spilling. Compare this with how many drops of soapy water will fit on a penny.

- Have your students write reports about what they did and what they discovered about liquids and drops.

Modifications for Kindergarten

- Consider having your students work only with water. If you want to use both water and oil, expand the lesson to two sessions.

- Allow more practice using the straws without water. If you think it will be too frustrating for your students to use the droppers, have them dip plastic "swizzle sticks" in the liquid and let the drops fall onto the waxed paper.

- Poll your students only on the shape of the drops. Have a few students report on other things they noticed.

Activity 4

Activity 4: Ocean in a Bottle Demonstration

Overview

Challenge your students to use what they have discovered in previous activities, as you construct a homemade version of a toy sold in many stores. Students enjoy tilting and shaking a bottle containing two liquids that don't mix. This demonstration also introduces the concept of "mixing," important for the last session in this unit, "Salad Dressing."

What You Need

- ☐ 3 clear, 8–10 ounce cups
- ☐ 1 squeeze bottle of blue food coloring
- ☐ 1 pint of water
- ☐ 1 pint of mineral oil, baby oil, or paraffin oil
- ☐ 1 clear, colorless tall bottle with a tight-fitting lid, such as tall baby food or juice jar, etc. Get more than one bottle if you'd like to make more than one ocean in a bottle. A 1-liter seltzer bottle, such as the one obtained for Activity 2, would also work well.
- ☐ 1 funnel if the bottles are narrow-mouthed
- ☐ a ziplock storage bag or other plastic bag large enough for each bottle you use
- ☐ 1 tray
- ☐ 1 large piece of white posterboard or paper (optional)

Many teachers prefer to present this demonstration as a hands-on participatory activity in which individual students or small groups of students make their own oceans in bottles. This works especially well with several students at a time.

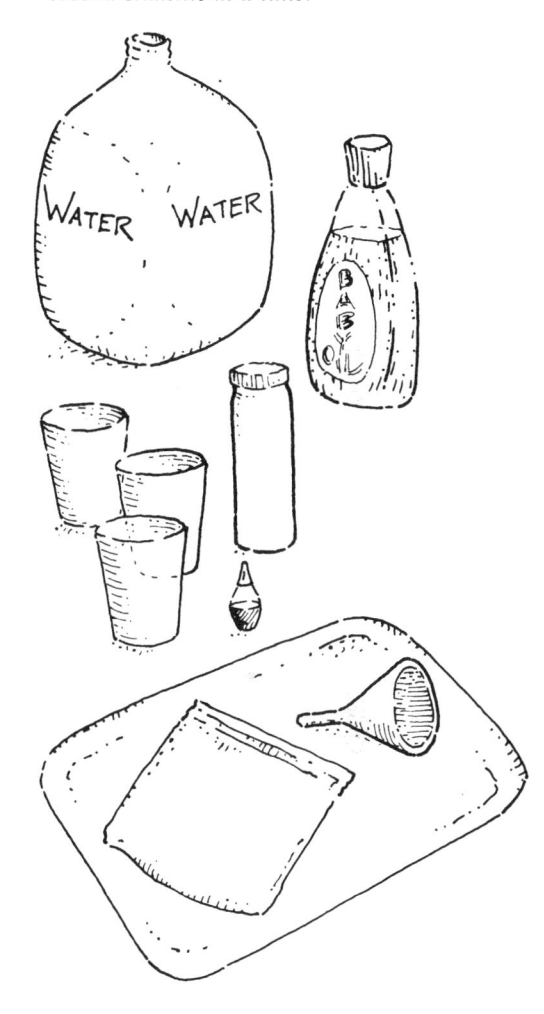

Using a larger bottle to make an ocean requires more oil and water but makes for a more interesting "wave-maker." Clear plastic two-liter soda bottles work well if you remove the labels and the black plastic bottoms. To remove the black plastic bottom from soda bottles: fill the soda bottle with water and freeze it. The plastic bottom will crack and can be removed easily when the ice thaws.

Or, you can also fill the bottle with very hot water—within several minutes the glue should soften and you can twist off the black base.

Activity 4   33

Getting Ready

1. Fill two cups one-third full with water. Fill the last cup one-third full with oil. Place these cups, the food coloring, the bottle, the mineral oil, and a ziplock bag on a tray. Put this tray near the demonstration area.

2. Choose a place where all your students will be able to see. Optional: A large piece of white posterboard or paper used as a background enhances visibility.

34   *Activity 4*

Demonstrating

1. Begin by telling the class that today they are going to mix some liquids together to see what happens.

2. Hold up one of the cups of water, moving it so the group can see how it flows. Tell the class to raise their hands if they think it is water. Call on several students to describe how it looks or moves like water. (Do not have students smell the liquids.)

3. Tell the students you will do a test on this liquid to get more evidence for whether or not it is plain water. Add two or three drops of food coloring to one cup and ask the students how the food coloring moved this time compared to how it moved in the liquids they tested in the "Swirling Colors" activity. Which does it move like most, the plain water or salt water? Reveal that it is plain water in the cup. Add more food coloring so the water becomes deep blue.

4. Hold up the second cup of water. Tell the students that it is also plain water. Explain that you will pour the colored water into the plain water. Ask the students to raise their hands if they think the two will mix and look like one liquid. Have others raise their hands if they think the two will not mix. Pour the two together and ask a student to take a close look and decide whether they look like one or two liquids now.

With older students you may want to say that liquids that mix are called miscible. *One way to remember the word is that it sounds like "mixable." Liquids that don't mix are considered* immiscible.

5. Hold up the third cup. Again, have students describe the liquid and say what they think it is. Explain that you will do another test to see if it is water. Tell the group that you will pour the colored water and this liquid together to see if they will mix. Pour the two together into the bottle.

6. Hold the mixture up for your students to examine. Ask one student to describe whether it looks like one liquid or two now. Remind the class of the "Raindrops and Oil Drops" activity. Ask what they noticed when they added oil to the water drops. Reveal that the third glass held mineral oil which will not mix with water. "Oil and water do not mix."

7. Screw the cap on the bottle very tightly. Hold the bottle on its side and tilt it. Ask the group if anyone can guess why this demonstration is called "an ocean in a bottle." [When rocked, the surface of the blue water looks like waves.] Place the bottle in a ziplock bag and seal it, explaining that they may play with it later, but they must keep it in the bag in case of spills. Depending on your students' level of interest, more "oceans in bottles" can be made at this time, or created later as a small group activity.

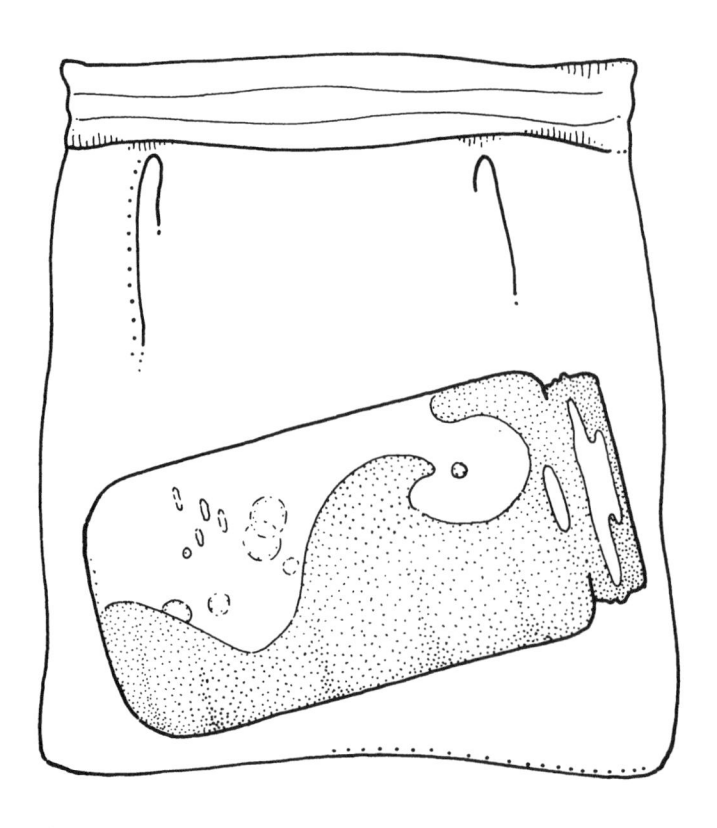

Going Further

- Demonstrate other safe mixtures such as:
  —colored water and rubbing alcohol
  —rubbing alcohol and oil
  —mineral oil and salad oil
  —vinegar and colored water
  (vinegar and oil will be mixed in the "Secret Salad Dressing" activity)
  —hair conditioner and water
  —dishwashing soap and oil

- Have students write short reports on what they noticed during the "Ocean in a Bottle" demonstration.

- Add small sea shells or sand to the "ocean in a bottle." The students can also tape paper fish or boats on the outside of the bottle to make an imaginary sea world.

You can also add small plastic animals (black ants are perfect) or glitter, or small aluminum foil boats to the liquids and watch them "surf on the waves." This can become an interesting extension as students predict and test various solids to see if they will float on the water layer.

Modifications for Kindergarten

Begin the activity by telling the children that you have some oil and water and that you're going to mix them together. Ask for predictions on whether or not they think the two liquids will mix.

38 *Activity 5*

Activity 5: Secret Salad Dressing

Overview

Your students investigate two liquids that don't mix—oil and vinegar. They then add seasonings to make their own secret salad dressings. They use a color-coded system for recording the formula of their salad dressing recipes so that it can be easily reproduced at home. This activity helps your students make connections between what happens in science lessons and things they might encounter at home.

Students enjoy developing their own secret recipes. A new GEMS guide, Secret Formulas, builds on this enthusiasm to explore cause-and-effect and gives students opportunities to create their own recipes for household items like toothpaste and ice cream. These activities, like this "secret salad dressing" activity, also help students improve their observation, measuring, and prediction skills.

What You Need

For the class:
- ☐ ½ gallon of salad oil
- ☐ 1 quart of cider or wine vinegar
- ☐ 1 clear, wide-mouthed container, 2–4 quart capacity (2–4 liters) A large glass jar, pitcher, or the bottom of a 2-liter clear, colorless soda bottle will work.
- ☐ 1 long-handled spoon
- ☐ 15 bowls or dishes, such as paper ice cream cups, margarine tubs, or cottage cheese containers
- ☐ 5 sheets of construction paper in 5 different colors
- ☐ approximately ½ cup (½ ounce) each of: oregano, sage, rosemary. If possible, obtain fresh herbs.
- ☐ approximately ½ cup (2 ounces) of pepper (coarsely ground)
- ☐ approximately ½ cup of salt
- ☐ 1 tray
- ☐ 1 roll of masking tape
- ☐ 1 pair of scissors
- ☐ newspaper to cover the tables
- ☐ a blank piece of paper, large enough to cover the label of the vinegar bottle
- ☐ a bucket if there is no access to a sink in your classroom
- ☐ dishwashing soap, sponges, and paper towels for cleanup

If your students can read and write the names of the seasonings, you don't need to color code them. Should you decide not to color code, you won't need construction paper or crayons, and you can skip those steps that involve these materials.

If the sides of the containers for seasonings can be written on, you can use colored markers rather than construction paper.

Loose-fitting lids can be a disaster in this activity. It is worth taking the time before class to make sure that each jar has a tight-fitting lid.

For each student:
- ☐ 1 4–8 ounce jar with a tight-fitting lid, such as a baby food or jam jar.
- ☐ 1 "Secret Salad Dressing" recipe sheet, master included, page 49
- ☐ 1 ziplock plastic bag, large enough to hold a 4–8 ounce jar
- ☐ crayons to match the colors of construction paper
- ☐ a pencil

Getting Ready

1. Duplicate one copy of the "Secret Salad Dressing" recipe sheet for each student. (Master included, page 49.)

2. Cut each sheet of construction paper into four strips. Attach a strip of one color to each of three bowls. Do the same for the remaining four colors, so you end up with a total of fifteen bowls, three labeled with blue, three labeled with yellow, etc. Save the remaining strip of each color for the chalkboard color-key in Step #7.

3. Divide the seasonings into the bowls; put the oregano into those with blue strips, the rosemary in the red, etc. Stack one of each kind of seasoning together to make a complete set of seasonings for each of the three stations. Place these three sets of seasonings on a tray.

4. Fill the large clear container with about three inches of oil.

Activity 5

```
□ oregano    _____
□ sage       _____
□ rosemary   _____
□ salt       _____
□ pepper     _____
```

5. Cover the label of the vinegar bottle with a piece of paper.

6. Put the container of oil, the vinegar bottle, the three stacks of seasonings, crayons to match the colors used, the spoon, and the data sheets next to where you plan to introduce the activity.

7. Copy the seasoning key from the recipe sheet on the chalkboard. Attach the remaining colored strips next to the names of the seasonings, corresponding to the color used to mark the bowls.

8. Have students help arrange the room by pushing desks together or moving tables so that there are three work stations. Cover each station with newspaper.

Activity 5

Observing and Comparing

1. Gather your students away from the three work stations. Tell the class that they will be using what they have learned to make something they can take home. Hold up the container of oil and gently shake it. Then hold up the vinegar bottle. Do not identify the liquids. Ask the class to describe how they are different. Ask one student to come up and smell the vinegar and the oil and tell the class what they smell like. (The other students will each get a chance to smell the liquids later.) After they have contrasted the two liquids, ask, "How are they the same?"

2. Tell the class you are going to pour the two liquids together. Have them raise their hands if they think that the two will mix and look like one liquid or whether they will make two layers. Pour half as much vinegar as oil into the container. Let another student volunteer stir the mixture. Have the class watch as the liquids settle and separate again.

3. Remind your students of previous observations by asking, "What liquids have you seen that do not mix?" At this point, you can identify the two liquids for the class and ask them how they could tell which liquid is on the top and which is on the bottom.

4. Ask if anyone knows what is made from both oil and vinegar. Reveal that you have made salad dressing—but something is missing. Show the class the seasonings. Demonstrate how to smell each herb by rubbing a piece between your fingers. Let them know that they will each get a chance to smell the herbs.

Secret Recipes

1. Tell the class that they will each get a chance to devise their own secret salad dressings to take home. Each student may decide what seasonings to put in, and how much of each seasoning to use. Explain that they will keep track of the ingredients and amounts on a secret recipe sheet. (Hold up a "Secret Salad Dressing" recipe sheet.)

Activity 5

Some teachers have chosen to color code recipe sheets for each student by sticking on colored dot stickers before handing out the recipe sheets.

2. Demonstrate how you would like the students to make their secret salad dressings and record the recipe. Explain that they will:

a. Write their names on the recipe sheets.

b. Color in the circle next to each seasoning, using the sample sheet on the chalkboard as a guide. Point out how the colors next to each name on the chalkboard match the colors on the bowls.

c. Choose a seasoning to smell. If they like it, they can put it into the empty jar. If they like it a lot, they can put in two or three pinches.

d. Ask the class, "How can I remember that I put in three pinches?" Show them how by writing "3" next to the name of that seasoning on the board. Ask them, "What should I write if I didn't put in any pinches?" ["0"] Go through each seasoning in the same way. Make sure that you vary the amounts; choose to leave out at least one seasoning, so that you can show how to indicate the amounts 1, 2, 3, and 0.

3. Tell the students that when they have finished adding seasonings and marking them on their recipe sheets, they should sit down at their seats. That will be their signal to you to come around and pour oil and vinegar in their jars.

On Their Own

1. Distribute the recipe sheets and have your students return to their seats to begin writing their names and coloring in the circles.

2. While they are working on this, distribute the empty jars with their lids and spread out bowls of seasonings at the three work stations. Circulate among the students, checking to make sure they are coloring in their seasoning key correctly, and answering any questions they may have.

3. Have your students begin adding the seasonings to their jars. Continue circulating among the stations to assist as needed.

4. As students finish and sit in their seats, come around to the tables with the tray of oil and vinegar. If possible, have an adult (or older student) help you fill each jar about half full with oil and a quarter full with vinegar, for about a 2:1 ratio. Cap each jar tightly and place it in a ziplock bag. Caution the students not to open the bag until they get home, to protect against spills. The mixture made during the demonstration can also be used to fill up their jars, as long as it is stirred well first.

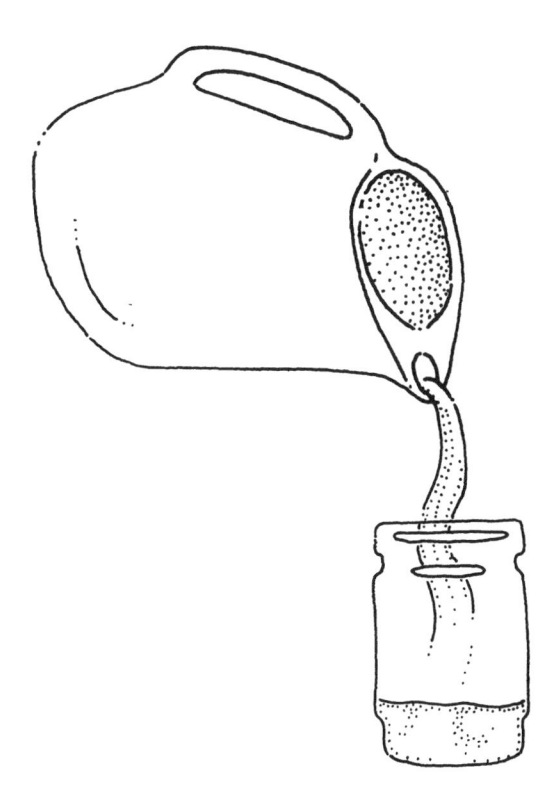

Activity 5

Concluding the Activity

1. Have students help collect all the bowls of seasonings and discard the newspaper.

2. Distribute a strip of masking tape to each of the students, asking them to write their names on the tape strips and then to stick them to their bags.

3. Have students observe the liquids in their salad dressings. Poll your students to find out whether they think the liquids did or did not mix. With older students, you may want to have them discuss the way the oil and vinegar mixed as compared to the way oil and water mixed in "Ocean in a Bottle."

4. To help summarize, collect two or three recipe sheets. Using the copy on the chalkboard, fill in the recipe used by one student. Have the class read it back to tell you how much of each seasoning was used. Ask, "Which seasoning did she use most?" "Which did she use the least?" "Did she use the same number of pinches for any two seasonings?" Do the same with another recipe.

5. Tell the students to take their salad dressings home and use them soon. When they run out, they will know how to make more by reading their secret recipes!

Going Further

1. Make a big "science salad" with lettuce and other vegetables for a class snack. Each student can try out his own secret salad dressing on his portion of salad.

2. Using the seasonings written on the chalkboard for the vertical axis, make a bar graph. On the bottom axis fill in the numbers 0 through 70 in intervals of five. Sum up the number of pinches that the whole class used for each seasoning by using the following procedure:

   a. Ask students to raise their hands if they used 1 pinch of oregano. Count the number and write it on the board.

   b. Have students raise their hands if they used 2 pinches of oregano. Count the responses and multiply the number by two.

   c. Do the same for three pinches. Multiply this number by three and write the total on the board.

   d. Determine the total number of pinches used. Use this total to fill in the bar graph.

Repeat this procedure for the remaining seasonings. When finished, ask:

- Which seasoning did the class like the most?

- Which seasoning did the class like the least?

- Were the same amounts used for any two seasonings?

3. Have the class research seasonings. They could find out the difference between herbs and spices, or make a display of various seasonings that they have classified. Herbs are generally the leaves from non-woody plants, such as oregano. Spices are usually derived from other parts of plants, such as the seeds and bark.

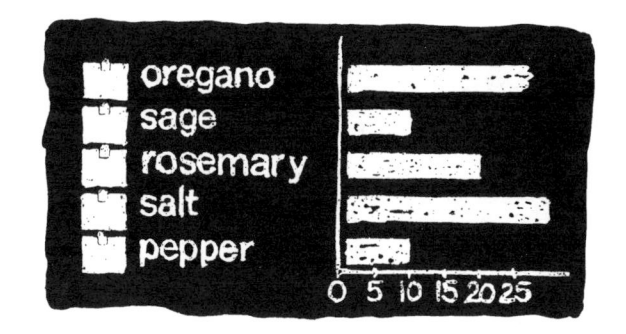

Modifications for Kindergarten

- Extend the lesson to two sessions.

    1. In the first, compare the liquids and demonstrate how to make salad dressing. Have your students prepare their record sheets by gluing a sample of each seasoning to their recipe sheets.

    2. During the second session, review how to make salad dressing and have the students make their own.

- Consider reducing the number of seasonings.

_____'s

Secret Salad Dressing Recipe

**Use this key to identify
the secret ingredients;**

_____   ◯   = salt

_____   ◯   = pepper

_____   ◯   = sage

_____   ◯   = rosemary

_____   ◯   = oregano

Plus oil and vinegar

Summary Outlines

Getting Ready Before Beginning the Unit

1. At least one month before beginning the unit, send letters home requesting donations of materials.

2. Look over the unit. Arrange to have assistance (aide, parent, grandparent, or older students).

Activity 1: Liquid Classification

Getting Ready Before the Activity

1. Assemble the materials.

2. Fill jars with liquids.

3. Write "LIQUID" on the board.

4. Optional: Place white background near discussion area.

Playing the Game

1. Introduce liquids as what students drink.

2. Ask how contents of two jars are the same.

3. Model game with 4–6 liquids.

4. Have students "guess your rule."

5. Play another round or two of game.

6. Conclude by asking what contents of all the jars have in common. For this unit, define liquid as "something that flows."

Subsequent Sessions

1. Review ways liquids were classified.

2. Play several rounds of game, having student volunteers classify.

Classification Levels

Continue playing game, adding variation and complexity or simplifying as appropriate.

Activity 2: Swirling Colors

Getting Ready Before the Activity

1. Assemble the materials.

2. Duplicate data sheets.

3. Fill containers with salt. Put a spoon and stir stick in each container.

4. Place data sheets and crayons at each desk.

5. Place three cups on every other desk, salt containers on remaining desks.

6. Fill two cups at the desks and the large container with water.

7. Put the large container of water, sugar, tablespoon, long spoon, food coloring, paper cups, a crayon, and sheet of paper near introduction area.

8. Sketch shape of large container of water on blank paper.

Demonstrating

1. Gather students away from desks.

2. Introduce challenge: How do colored drops move through various liquids?

3. Demonstrate how to measure a level spoon as you add 8 tablespoons sugar to the water in the large container.

4. Stir until sugar is dissolved and have students tell you when water is still. Explain that this is sugar water.

5. Add a drop of food coloring. Emphasize importance of not jiggling, stirring, or blowing on the liquid.

6. Use students' descriptions to draw what happened to the drop in sugar water.

7. Tell students they will compare how colored drops move through plain, salty, and bubbly water.

8. Explain procedural details:

    a. Work in pairs. One person measures and stirs, other has cups.
    b. Both draw what they see.
    c. First cup for plain water, middle cup for salt water.
    d. Begin drawing as soon as drop is added.

9. Students return to seats to write names on papers.

Observing and Recording

1. Have students place hands over middle cup. The measurers add four teaspoons of salt to middle cup and stir.

2. Collect equipment. Add a drop of color to each plain-water cup. Remind students to draw immediately.

3. When salt water stops moving, add drops of color.

4. Pour seltzer water and add food coloring.

A Refreshing Finale

1. Empty cups into bucket.

2. Draw three cups on board. Have students describe what happened in each as you draw. How are they different?

3. Add lemons to sugar water and distribute cups of lemonade. Enjoy!

Activity 3: Raindrops and Oil Drops

Getting Ready Before the Activity

1. Assemble the materials.

2. Cut squares of wax paper and newspaper for each student.

3. Cut drinking straws in half, remove wrappers.

4. Practice using straw-eyedropper.

5. Move pairs of desks together and cover with newspaper.

6. Put square of waxed paper on each paper plate.

7. Fill containers with water and place one on each pair of desks. Fill clear cup with water.

8. Fill bottle caps with oil and place on tray.

9. Place plates, straws, cups of oil and water, oil bottle, and newspaper squares in introduction area.

Demonstrating the Dropper

1. Gather students away from desks.

2. Have them compare oil and water.

3. Introduce challenge: to compare single drops of each liquid.

4. Demonstrate making a drop using straw dropper.

5. Show how to bring head to table level to view drops from side.

6. Distribute straws and practice using droppers as many times as needed.

7. Draw possible shapes of drops from side view on board.

Investigating Water Drops

1. Have students return to desks.

2. Circulate, helping students and asking questions.

3. Bring students back to discussion area and poll for observations.

Investigating Oil Drops

1. Introduce challenge of comparing oil and water and seeing what happens when they mix.

2. Send students back to desks to investigate.

3. Distribute new droppers and caps of oil.

4. Circulate, helping students and asking questions.

5. Bring students back to discussion area to share observations.

Activity 4: Ocean in a Bottle Demonstration

Getting Ready Before the Activity

1. Fill 2 cups ⅓ full with water. Fill a third cup ⅓ full with mineral oil. Put these with bottle, food coloring, ziplock bag, and mineral oil on tray.

2. Optional: Place white background near discussion area.

Demonstrating

1. Tell students they are going to mix liquids to see what happens.

2. Keeping its identity a mystery, have students describe the water. See how a colored drop moves through it. Reveal its identity.

3. Identify the contents of the second cup as water. Pour colored water into clear water. Does it mix?

4. Have students describe and guess identity of contents of third cup.

5. Pour contents of two cups in bottle. Ask students if liquids mixed.

6. Cap bottle and have students observe movement of "ocean in a bottle." Put in bag and let students play with it.

Summary Outlines 55

Activity 5: Secret Salad Dressing

Getting Ready Before the Activity

1. Duplicate recipe sheets.

2. Color code each set of bowls with construction paper.

3. Fill each color of bowl with a different seasoning.

4. Fill large clear container with about 3" of oil.

5. Cover vinegar bottle label.

6. Put container of oil, spoon, bottles of oil and vinegar, 3 sets of bowls with seasonings, 5 crayons, and recipe sheets in introduction area.

7. Copy names of seasonings on board and tape matching construction paper color next to names.

8. Push desks together into three work areas and cover with newspaper.

Observing and Comparing

1. Gather students away from work stations.

2. Introduce challenge: to use what they know about liquids to make something to take home.

3. Have students compare oil and vinegar: How are they the same and different?

4. Ask students if liquids will mix. Try it.

5. Ask what liquids they have seen that make two layers. Reveal identity of liquids in each layer.

6. Tell students this is salad dressing, but it needs seasonings. Show how to smell herbs.

Secret Recipes

1. Explain that they will each make their own salad dressing and keep track of the seasonings they used.

2. Demonstrate procedure:

    a. Write name on recipe sheet.
    b. Color circles next to each seasoning name.
    c. Smell and add seasonings they like.
    d. Record number of pinches used for each seasoning.
    e. When finished, sit in seats to get oil and vinegar.

On Their Own

1. Have students return to work stations.

2. Distribute recipe sheets.

3. Distribute jars, lids, and seasonings.

4. Students write names and color recipe sheets.

5. Students choose and record seasonings.

6. As students finish, fill jars ½ full with oil and ¼ full with vinegar. Cap lids tightly and seal jars in plastic bags.

Concluding the Activity

1. Students collect seasonings and throw away newspaper.

2. Distribute masking tape strips for students to label bags.

3. Students observe and compare liquids in their salad dressings with those used in "Ocean in a Bottle."

4. Collect recipe sheets and record one or two on chalkboard. Have students tell you how much of each seasoning was used.

Assessment Suggestions

Selected Student Outcomes

1. Students describe and compare the qualities that make one liquid different from another, and those that make them similar.

2. Students improve their ability to classify substances according to their attributes.

3. Students can articulate that some liquids mix while others do not.

Built-In Assessment Activities

Classifying Liquids: In Activity 1: Liquid Classification, students play a Guess My Rule classification game. If this activity is repeated at the end of the unit or later in the school year, teachers can look for improvements in students' ability to observe, compare, and classify liquid attributes. (Outcomes 1, 2)

Some Liquids Mix—Others Don't: In the opening demonstrations of Activity 4: Ocean in a Bottle and Activity 5: Secret Salad Dressing, students guess whether the various liquids might mix. After the liquids are poured together, the children are encouraged to explain what happened. The teacher can see how students articulate their guesses and explanations. (Outcome 3)

Additional Assessment Ideas

Classifying Other Things: A "Going Further" activity for Liquid Classification has students classify various materials such as leaves, attribute blocks, fruits, vegetables, or shoes. This gives the teacher an opportunity to observe how students can apply classification skills in new situations. (Outcome 2)

Mystery Liquids: In the "Going Further" activity for Swirling Colors, students observe how drops of color move through mystery liquids. The teacher can observe how students use the results from the initial experiment to determine the identity of the mystery liquid. (Outcome 1)

Shipwrecked!: Students are asked to help a pirate determine which liquids are saltwater and which are freshwater without tasting them. This could be a writing assignment. (Outcome 1)

Imaginary Liquids: Ask students to draw an imaginary liquid and to think of a name for it. Tell them that they are the only people who know the special properties of their liquid. First have the students in small groups each tell you about their liquids; then, ask them to tell you how the liquids are similar to each other, and how they are different. (Outcome 1)

Resources

Classroom Activities:

- Full Option Science System (FOSS), *Solids and Liquids* module, for Grades 1 and 2, developed at the Lawrence Hall of Science and published by and available from Encyclopaedia Britannica Educational Corporation, (800) 554-9862.

- SCIIS, Science Curriculum Improvement Study, Delta Education, Nashua, NH

    Material Objects
    Interaction and Systems
    Subsystems and Variables

- Elementary Science Study, New York, McGraw-Hill Book Co. 1978.

    Attribute Games and Problems
    Drops, Streams, and Containers
    Ice Cubes
    Colored Solutions

In this FOSS module, with four main activities, students describe properties of solid objects, then use them in construction projects. They investigate the properties of particulate solids (cornmeal, beans, rice) and liquids (water, corn syrup, oil) and compare their behaviors. After observing solid/liquid and liquid/liquid interactions, students investigate toothpaste to determine if it is a solid or liquid.

Home Experiments:

Originally intended for home use, many of the activity ideas presented in the following books can be adapted for classroom use and to the level of your students. (See "Helpful Hints for Hands-On Science in the Classroom," page 61.) These books include ideas about ways to use liquids to make "scientific artwork" and science snacks.

Cobb, Vicki, J.P. Lippincott, Company:

Science Experiments You Can Eat (1972)
More Science Experiments You Can Eat (1979)
Gobs of Goo (1983)

Allison, Linda and David Katz. *Gee Wiz! How to mix art and science or the art of thinking scientifically*, Yolla Bolly Press, 1983.

Literature Connections

Some of the books listed here as good literature connections to *Liquid Explorations* focus on **water**—what you can do with water, where it can be found, its properties, its different phases (fog, snow, steam, etc.), the water cycle, and how water is purified so we can drink it. You and your students may have other favorites.

Other books focus on **classification**, relating especially to Activity 1: Liquid Classification. There is also one book with a section about **salad dressings** that relates nicely to Activity 5: Secret Salad Dressing.

We also included a book in which various liquids (with various attributes) are mixed to create a mysterious liquid potion with magical powers. This and other books with a fantasy twist are great ways to unleash your students' imaginations as they use their understanding of **liquids and liquid properties** to weave and follow stories.

You may also want to refer to *Once Upon A GEMS Guide: Connecting Young People's Literature to Great Explorations in Math and Science* (also known as the GEMS literature handbook) for listings of other related books, especially those listed under the GEMS guides *Involving Dissolving, Oobleck, River Cutters, Solids, Liquids, and Gases,* and the science theme of "Matter."

About Water
by Laurent deBrunhoff
Random House, New York, 1980
Out of print
Grades: Preschool–2
> Barbar the elephant finds a world of water in this tiny book—water to drink, to bathe in, to boat on, to dive in, to feed a fountain, and even to use as a mirror.

The Car Washing Street
by Denise Lewis Patrick: pictures by John Ward
Tambourine Books, New York, 1993
Grades: preK–2
> This book shows water "doing" many things, uses a lot of "wet" vocabulary, and finishes up with ice treats. Also notable for multicultural illustrations.

Elliot's Extraordinary Cookbook
by Christina Bjork: illustrated by Lena Anderson
R&S Books/Farrar, Straus & Giroux, New York. 1990
Grades: 4–7
> With the help of his upstairs neighbor, Elliot cooks wonderful food, and investigates what's healthy and what's not so healthy. He finds out about proteins, carbohydrates, and the workings of the small intestine. He learns about the history of chickens, how cows produce milk, and how live yeast is used in rye bread. His friend shows him how to grow bean sprouts, and he sews an apron. On page 26 are two recipes for salad dressing that relate to the Secret Salad Dressing activities in the GEMS guide.

Everybody Needs a Rock
by Byrd Baylor; illustrated by Peter Parnall
Aladdin Books, New York. 1974
Grades: K–5
> What are the qualities to consider in selecting the perfect rock for play and pleasure? In finding out, the properties of color, size, shape, texture, and smell are discussed in a way that you'll want to rush out and find a rock of your own. Nice introduction or follow-up to a discussion of the properties of solids.

Gorky Rises
by William Steig
Farrar, Straus & Giroux, New York. 1980.
Grades: 2–5
> When Gorky's parents leave the house, he sets up a laboratory at the kitchen sink and mixes up a liquid mixture with a few secret ingredients, drops of his mother's perfume, and his father's cognac! The liquid proves to have magical properties that allow him to fly over the world. Although the format is a picture book, the content makes it usable for older students. Nice connection to the attributes and properties of liquids, with a fantasy twist.

Harriet's Halloween Candy
by Nancy Carlson
Puffin/Penguin, New York. 1982
Grades: Preschool–3
> Harriet learns the hard way that sharing her Halloween candy makes her feel much better than eating it all herself. In the process, she sorts, classifies, and counts her candy. Fun activity to do at Halloween or with any food items. A good connection to the sorting and classifying game in Session 1 of Liquid Explorations.

The Magic School Bus at the Waterworks
by Joanna Cole; illustrated by Bruce Degen
Scholastic, New York. 1986
Grades: K–6
> Ms. Frizzle, the "strangest teacher in school," takes her class on a field trip to the waterworks. First, they journey to the clouds where the class rains, each kid inside his own raindrop. Then they end up experiencing the water purification system from the inside, traveling through the mixing basin, settling basin, filter, and through the pipes to emerge from a faucet. Evaporation, the water cycle, and filtration are just a few of the concepts explored in this whimsical field trip.

Rain Drop Splash
by Alvin Tresselt; illustrated by Leonard Weisgard
Lothrop, Lee & Shepard, New York. 1946
Mulberry Books/William Morrow, New York. 1990
Grades: K–3

> Raindrops fall to make puddles. Puddles become larger and larger to form ponds. Ponds overflow into brooks that lead to lakes. The rainstorm continues, falling on plants and animals, making mud, flooding a road. The last scene leads to the ocean, when at last the rain stops and the sun emerges.

Shoes
by Elizabeth Winthrop; illustrated by William Joyce.
Harper & Row, New York. 1986
Grades: K–2

> A survey of the many kinds of shoes in the world concludes that the best of all are the perfect natural shoes that are your feet. Great to read before doing a survey of shoes, sorting and classifying a group of real shoes. or with any other sorting and classifying activities.

The Snowy Day
by Ezra Jack Keats
Viking, New York. 1962
Grades: Preschool–2

> Peter goes for a walk on a snowy day. He makes different patterns in the snow with his feet, a stick, and then his whole body. He tries to save a snowball in his pocket but is disappointed when it melts. That night Peter dreams that the sun melted all the snow outside, but when he wakes up, it's snowing again!

Splash! All About Baths
by Susan K. Buxbaum and Rita G. Gelman; illustrated by Maryann Cocca-Leffler
Little, Brown, and Co., Boston. 1987
Grades: K–6

> Before he bathes, Penguin answers his animal friends' questions about baths. "What shape is water?" "Why do soap and water make you clean?" "What is a bubble?" "Why does the water go up when you get in?" "Why do some things float and others sink?" and other questions. Answers to questions are both clear and simple. Received the American Institute of Physics Science Writing Award.

Two Bad Ants
by Chris Van Allsburg
Houghton Mifflin, Boston, 1988
Grades: Preschool–4

> This beautifully illustrated book about two ants in search of sugar provides opportunities to further discuss a liquid as something that flows, and to see that some substances, such as sugar, which also flow or pour, are in fact made up of tiny crystal solids.

Very Last First Time
by Jan Andrews; illustrated by Ian Wallace
Atheneum/Macmillan, New York. 1985
Grades: 2–4

This entrancing book tells the story of the Inuit girl Eva who walks for the first time in a sea-floor cavern under the frozen ocean ice. When the tide is out she and her mother come to gather mussels and Eva goes below the ice. When she stumbles, her candle goes out and the tide starts to come in, roaring louder, while the ice shrieks and creaks. Terrified at first, Eva recovers, and eventually finds her way to the surface and her waiting mother and the moonlight. Although the book does not scientifically explain the freezing of the top of the sea or the action of the tides, you and your class may want to discuss these questions: Why does only the top part of the water freeze? Why does the ice stay intact even when the water underneath it goes out with the tide? The images of Eva on the sea floor beneath the ice are unique and fascinating, enhanced by the eerie purple tones of the illustrations. The descriptive language and Eva's intense interest in nature exemplify excellent scientific observation skills.

Water's Way
by Lisa W. Peters; illustrated by Ted Rand
Arcade Publishing/ Little Brown and Co., New York. 1991
Grades: K–3

"Water has a way of changing" inside and outside Tony's house, from clouds to steam to fog and other forms. Innovative illustrations show the changes in the weather outside while highlighting water changes inside the house.

Water Is Wet
by Sally Cartwright
McCann & Geoghegan, Inc., New York, 1973.

Highlights observations and descriptions of water for young children.

Water on Your Street
by Seymour Simon
Holiday House, New York, 1974

A wonderful read-aloud book investigating where the water in your sink comes from and where it goes when it leaves. The book includes activity suggestions.

Whose Hat Is That?
by Ron Roy; photographs by Rosemarie Hausherr
Clarion Books/Ticknor and Fields, New York. 1987
Grades: Preschool–3

Text and photographs portray the appearance and function of eighteen types of hats including a top hat, a jockey's cap, and a football helmet. The children and adults modeling the hats represent a rainbow of peoples. Makes a nice connection to classification activites in Session 1.

Helpful Hints For Hands-On Science in the Classroom

- **If you can, get a helper!** Though assistance is not always necessary, if you are doing something for the first time, have many materials to distribute, are concerned about the possibility of spills, or want to be able to listen and respond to questions, then you will greatly appreciate the extra help. If you can't enlist an aide, or a parent, consider signing on a few reliable fifth or sixth grade students. If you have a regularly scheduled science time, you could set up a revolving team of older helpers so every session is covered. You, your students, and the helpers will all benefit from the experience.

- **If possible, hold listening and discussion parts of the activities away from the place where students do their experiments.** Students have a difficult time listening if there are materials distracting them. Find a good place to gather your students for these times. A rug area or a reading corner are good possibilities. Alternatively, you may gather the students around your desk or around a large table. If none of these areas are available, plan to set up materials on trays so you can easily pick up materials before the discussion.

  Once students are involved in an activity, it is usually better not to give new group directions or ask questions of the entire class. Instead, circulate among the students, interacting with small groups.

- **Reduce distribution of materials during the activity to a minimum.** Plan to do activities that involve distributing many materials just after students have left the room for recess, lunch, or another class. Let students know before they leave where you want them to meet when they return. Set up the materials at their desks while they are out of the room.

  Alternatively, arrange all of the materials for a team of six to eight students on individual trays. Have a representative from each team distribute and collect these trays.

- **Begin a collection of multi-purpose, waterproof materials,** such as milk carton bottoms, unbreakable containers with lids, plastic spoons, plastic coffee stir sticks, and styrofoam egg cartons for your science activities throughout the year.

Jars: Baby food jars are excellent because they do not break easily and have tight-fitting lids. Other good types of jars include: jam, pickle, herring, artichoke, or other small jars with tight-fitting lids.

Good containers for salt and seasonings: paper ice cream cups (ask at the local ice cream parlor), plastic or paper bowls, margarine tubs, take-out soup bowls, yogurt cups, etc.

Stir sticks: popsicle sticks, plastic coffee stirrers

- **Collect the materials you need for the unit early!** At least one month before beginning the unit, look over the materials list and decide which you can get from the school and which you already have. Many of the materials, such as the jars, may be collected by the students from their families. Feel free to copy the letter to parents that appears on page 63, and add to it any other materials you need.

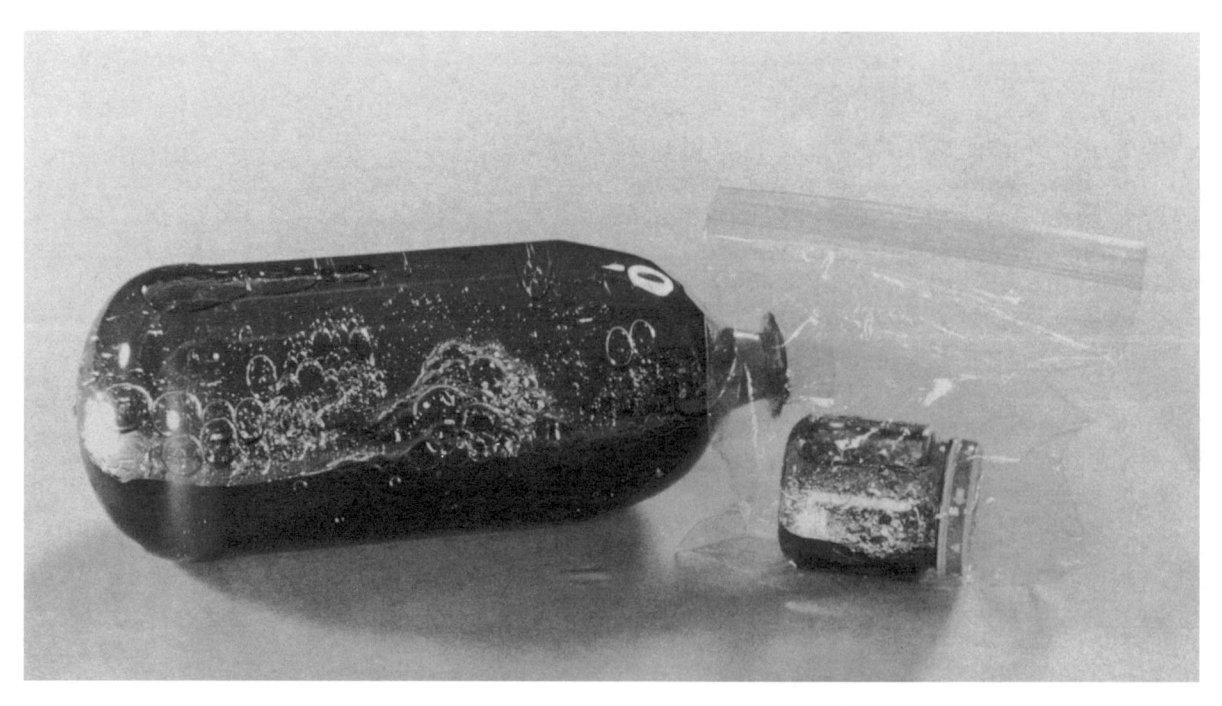

Dear Parents,

Your child's class will soon begin a unit on liquids. They will learn about how various liquids are different and how they are the same. They will be conducting experiments and making things with liquids, while learning and practicing important science skills. There are many things that we need for this project, so we are asking for your help. Please see if you have any of the following items, or if you know of others who do. We will need our materials by _____.

- baby food jars (or jars of similar size **with lids**)

- tall, narrow, clear jars or bottles **with tight-fitting lids**

- old newspapers

- high-rimmed bottle caps (such as those from vinegar jugs or screw-top bottles)

- clear, colorless, 2-liter-capacity soda bottles

-

-

It will be appreciated if all your donations have been cleaned. Do you know anyone with a baby? Are there people where you work who might help? Please pass this note on to others!

Thank you very much for your help,

Helpful Hints **67**

plain water

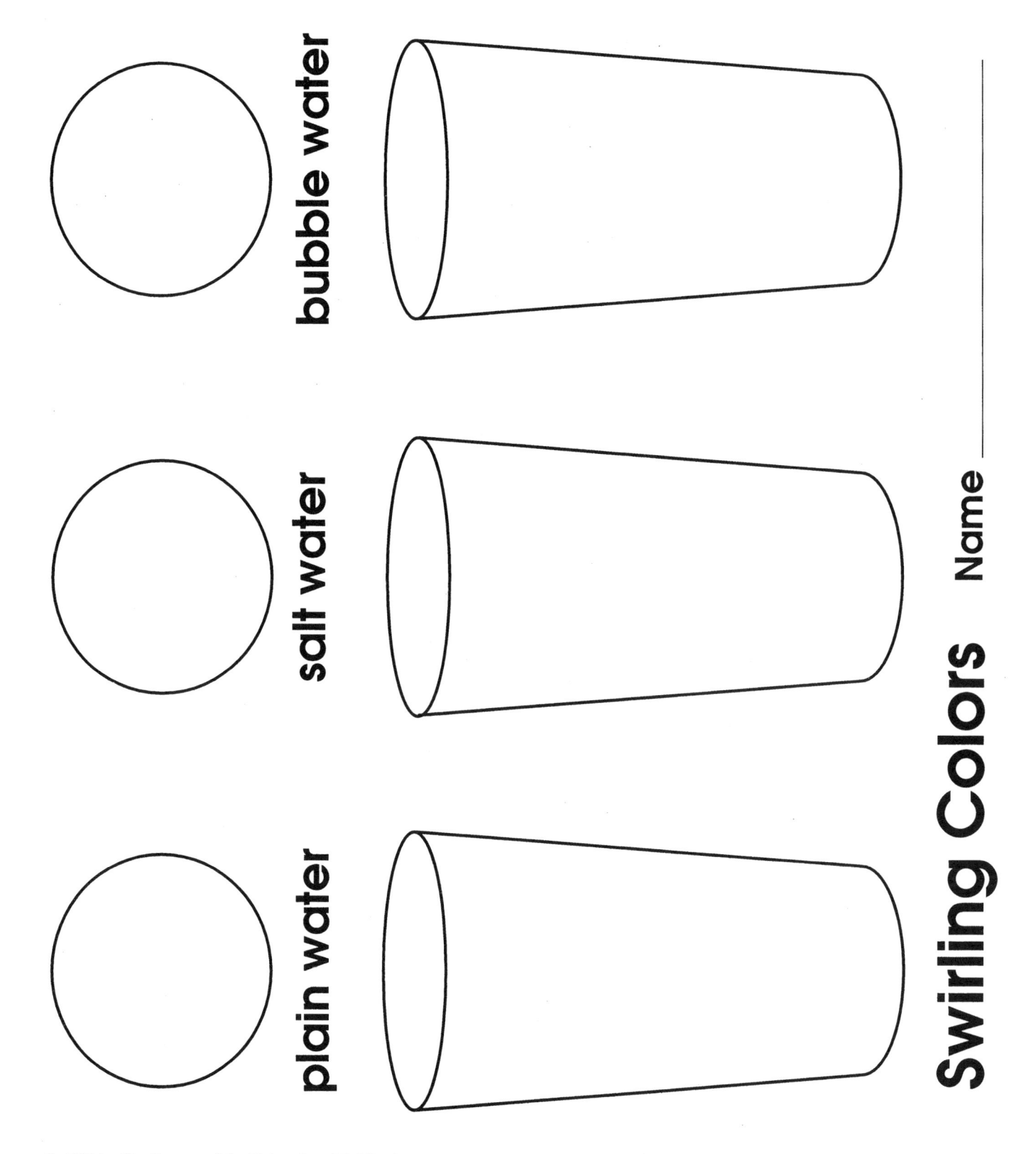

salt water

bubble water

Swirling Colors Name _____

© 1987 by The Regents of the University of California
  LHS—Great Explorations in Math and Science: *Liquid Explorations*

_____'s

Secret Salad Dressing Recipe

Use this key to identify
the secret ingredients;

_____ ◯ = salt

_____ ◯ = pepper

_____ ◯ = sage

_____ ◯ = rosemary

_____ ◯ = oregano

Plus oil and vinegar

© 1987 by The Regents of the University of California
LHS—Great Explorations in Math and Science: *Liquid Explorations*